LIGHT

Creation and Evolution in the Bible

ELYSE CURTIS, Ph. D.

Astral Projections
New York, NY

For information address:
Astral Projections
191 Claremont Ave., Suite 53
New York, NY 10027

1st Printing 1997

Printed in the USA

Library of Congress Catalog Card Number 97-93213

ISBN 0-9657282-0-X

Cover Design and Illustrations by Elyse Curtis
Photos by Sharda Devi

Excerpt from WHO'S WHO IN EGYPTIAN MYTHOLOGY
Copyright (c) 1978 by Anthony S. Mercatante. First Edition pub-
lished by Clarkson N. Potter, Inc./Publishers, New York 1978.
Reprinted here with permission of the author's agent, Susan Ann
Protter Literary Agent.

To all seekers of Light

Other Works by the Author
(from Astral Projections)

Metaphors, Dreams and The Revelation
(How life paths are revealed through personal symbols)

There Are No Coincidences (Autobiography)

The Song Divine:
The Transcendental Nature of Early Twentieth Century Love Songs.

Behind the Veil:
A Study of the Birth Caul as an Indication of Innate Intuitive Abilities

Ballad of The Revelation
(The Revelation of John the Divine in Verse)

Body, Mind, Spirit Connections (Collected Essays)

Who Was Who:
A Past-Life Directory Based on the Edgar Cayce Discourses

The Seven Stars (A Musical of The Revelation)

Act Five, The Perils of Paul
(Musical of the Misadventures of the Apostle Paul)

Mad Blake (Musical of the life and work of William Blake)

Good Intentions (Play with music)

Viva Aida! (Contemporary Musical Adapted from Verdi's opera)

Eugene Grandet (Dramatic adaptation of Balzac's novel)

Where Is Soul Mate? (Musical)

Mass Mass (Contemporary Mass)

Gentle Spirit (Biblical and Inspirational Songbooks I & II)

CONTENTS

Preface

"It seems to me absurd, to doubt that a man may be an ardent Theist and an evolutionist." - Charles Darwin, May 7, 1879

According to the literal interpretation of translations of the Bible, creation of the universe took place around 6,000 years ago and humans were created on the sixth day of the process. In contrast, the most popular currently held scientific theory is that the universe was created 15 or 20 billion years ago and is still expanding. The planet Earth is also thought to be around four-and-a-half billion years old and human-like fossils thought to be millions of years old have been unearthed. The dilemma created by this schism between the theories of creation and evolution and the Biblical account was addressed in 1996 by Pope John II. He acknowledged that new information and scientific research leads to the "recognition of the theory of evolution as more than just a hypothesis," but affirmed that "the spiritual soul is immediately created by God" (N.Y. Times 10/27/96). However, the time gap between the theories of creation and evolution and the Biblical creation as translated appears to be as irreconcilable as day and night. Yet, there is a close resemblance between the two versions. Since a certain harmony exists between the process of creation in the Biblical story and the theories, is there also evidence in the Bible in support of the time span and the existence of prehistoric hominid? When carefully examined, the Bible is found to contain such evidence, and many other details about humankind's origin and relationship to the universe, that greatly narrows the gap between science, mythology, and religion.

Elyse Curtis, Ph.D.

From the Zohar

... every word of the Law [the Torah] holds an exalted meaning and a sublime mystery.

... David had this in mind when he said: 'Open Thou, my eyes, that I may behold wondrous things out of Thy Law' (i.e., what is hidden under the cloak of the Law - Ps. 119.18)

... If the Law consisted of nothing but ordinary words and recitals, like the words of Esau, Hagar, Laban, Balaam's ass and Balaam himself, why should it have been called the Law of Truth, the perfect Law, the faithful testimony of God? Why should the wise man deem it more precious than gold and pearls? But it is not so. Every word conceals a most elevated meaning; every recital contains more than the events it seems to contain. And this higher and more holy Law is the true Law (Franck 80-81).

Introduction

A description of the initial movement of the Spirit of God that brought forth light could literally fit the currently held theory of the explosion of a "giant atom" that precipitated creation. And the seemingly conflicting statements in the Bible, "world without end," (Isa. 45.17) and "heaven and earth shall pass away," (Mark 13.31) can describe an expanding universe with the birth and death of stars. To date, the theory does not reach beyond the initial explosion to the origin of the "giant atom." Its presupposed existence is accepted on faith based on what exists now. And neither does the Bible explain the origin of God, whose omnipresent existence is accepted on faith. Both versions of creation begin with the premise that the first cause was. If the story of creation in Genesis were written in current scientific terms, it would sound similar to the theories. A millennium from now it would probably have to be re-worded to conform to the idiom of the future and possibly new knowledge. Fortunately, the language used in the Bible is basic enough to survive man's evolving semantics and growing conscious knowledge. The complicated process of creation is so simplified that it will be understood in all ages. Words such as heaven and earth have retained the same symbolic meanings that they had when the Book of Genesis was compiled, and day and night still represent opposites.

As any given word in the modern languages can be defined with a variety of synonyms that can often be used to define entirely different words (i.e., darkness can be defined as absence of light, wickedness, secrecy, and ignorance), so the individual words of the original language also conveyed varied meanings. The words used to translate the Bible from the original, when not confirmed by repeated use in similar situations where there could be no doubt of their meanings, were chosen at the discretion of the translators based on their own persuasions. This is witnessed by the variations in the six popular versions of the Bible that seldom agree on the interpretations of crucial words. As an example, Genesis 49.22 is translated:

> Joseph is a fruitful vine - The Masoretic Text (MT)
> (Hebrew Scriptures)

9

Joseph is a wild colt - The New American Bible (NAB)
(Catholic Bible)

Joseph is a fruitful bough - King James Version (KJV &
RSV) (Protestant)

Joseph is a disciplined son - Lamsa Bible (LB) (The
Peshitta - Aramaic)

Joseph is a fruitful tree - The New English Bible (NEB)
(Protestant)

Joseph is like a wild donkey - Good News Bible (GNB)
(Today's Version)

While the fruitful vine, the fruitful bough, and the fruitful tree are in accord, and the wild colt and the wild donkey are in accord, they can convey different symbolic meanings as can the disciplined son.

The Bible is allegorical as well as literal, and it speaks to man's body, mind and spirit. Specifically, it is the history of the children of Israel. Symbolically, it is the story of mankind collectively in the earth and individually in the body. The allegorical aspects of the Bible are referred to by Paul in Galatians 4.24, in the "Expositions of Scriptures" in the *Dead Sea Scriptures* (Gaster 299-331) and in the *Kabbalah* and *Zohar.*

The three levels of the Bible meld into one another so inconspicuously that separating them becomes a challenge. If the symbology of the Bible is considered, the words chosen in translation will be consistent with the literal and allegorical levels.

Like current books, the Bible does not explain what was accepted as common knowledge when it was written. For instance, there is no mention in Genesis of the creation of angels, sons of God, Cherubim or Nephilim, by those names, they simply appear without explanation of their origin. So, in order to gain a complete picture of the Biblical creation, it is necessary to glean the information from other passages in the Bible.

Some statements in the Bible that were enigmatic just a very short time ago are more clearly understood now that our knowledge has increased. The more we learn, the more accurate the Bible appears to be. The major difference between the theories of creation and evolution and the Biblical story is that in the theories intelligence, or consciousness, is the end product of creation and in the Bible it is the beginning.

Prologue
In The Beginning Gods...

The scientific theory of creation begins with the explosion of the primal substance, the "giant atom." The Biblical story begins with the creator of the primal substance. The name given to this creator, who is represented in the Bible as the All, the Omnipresent Consciousness, the Infinite Mind, is Elohiym, which is translated as God. However, Elohiym[1] (which is also the word for goddess) is the plural of Elowahh: "a deity or the Deity," from El: "strength, mighty, Almighty." If the first line were translated according to the original, it would read, "In the beginning[2] Gods..."

Though the singular translation of Elohiym diminishes the concept of pluralism, which would have made it similar to other creation "myths," it also diminishes the idea of a triune (three aspects of the Infinite Mind) and does not convey the same idea as the original.

The Primal Substance

Just as man, who is an infinitesimal speck in the universe, first creates a plan at the unseen level, on the plane of intellect, then assembles the materials and makes his creation, so the invisible God, the Omnipresent "Mind," created a plan on the unseen level and assembled the materials before what had been created as idea was made manifest:

> Through faith we understand that the worlds
> were framed by the word of God, so that
> things which are seen were not made by things
> which do appear (Heb. 11.3).

The worlds that would be framed would be made from things that are invisible. The complete first verse is:

> In the beginning GOD created the heavens

---

[1] Unless otherwise indicated "God" in Genesis is the plural, Elohiym.
[2] Reshiyth: "first in place, time, order or rank," from rosh: "the head."

and the earth (Gen. 1.1).

Since the actual manifestation of heaven and earth does not occur until after the light is brought forth, it is the substances of which they will be composed that are created, or envisioned, in the first verse.

Heaven: shamayim, is also plural. It is defined as: "to be lofty, the sky," and "air." As air, heaven is envisioned as a gaseous mixture. Air is also symbolic of the mental realm, and heaven is often described as a pleasant state of imagination experienced when one's "head is in the clouds." Earth: erets, is defined as probably meaning, "to be firm." The planet Earth is composed of some 92 substances called elements. The earth was first envisioned as substances not organized into a particular form that would become firm:

> And the earth was without form, and void: and darkness was upon the face of the deep (Gen. 1.2).

At this point, the Biblical story is at the stage of the supposed "giant atom." If a comparison exists here with the "atom," the clue would be in face. There are four words translated as face in the Bible. Face here is paneh, "the face (as the part that turns)" from panah, "to turn." The deep, as the center, is the nucleus, and the face, as the part that turns, can be compared to the electrons that orbit around a nucleus to form an atom. However, the deep more closely fits the description of a "black hole." As such, it would not be the beginning of all creation, but a new beginning in a continuous universe, because a "black hole" is supposed to be the final stage of a huge star. This would also account for the existence of carbon, oxygen, iron, gold, lead, copper, uranium, etc., the elements that can only be explained by the birth and death of stars. (The expanding universe theory only accounts for the presence of hydrogen and helium.) The darkness that was on the face of the deep: choshek, "the dark, obscurity, ignorance," also means "wickedness, evil, sorrow, misery, death and destruction," which suggests some pre-existent state that was somehow out of harmony. Until recently, "black holes" were considered passive. The latest theory is that they might be the most active and explosive objects in the universe (even though they are unseen), and that in their final stages they produce violent explosions.

Whether a "giant atom," "black hole," or something else, this pre-existent condition, was equivalent to the Biblical deep: tehom, "an abyss (as a surging mass of water) from huwm: "to make an uproar, or agitate greatly." As such, the deep can be described as the unseen level, a sort of "cosmic sub-unconscious," a state below the surface, the hidden recesses of the "Infinite Mind" in which rested the unspoken word, as active imagery, or "idea," for creation of the cosmos.

In the Hindu creation story in the Rig Veda (X.129) before the existence of being or non-being, before the existence of night or day, there was only darkness hidden by darkness and covered by the formless void and deep unfathomable water. All was that One thing, which breathed by its own nature, and All that existed was indistinctive chaos. The One was born of the power of warmth. Desire entered the water in the beginning as the seed of spirit, the first thought.

> and the Spirit of GOD moved upon the face
> of the waters (Gen. 1.2).

The Spirit of God represents the activating agent that is not identified in the "big bang" theory. Spirit: ruwach, is defined as "wind" by resemblance "breath," and is also translated as "mind." Wind, or breath, as air, would symbolically be in the heavenly, or mental/spiritual realm. As the force of God, the Spirit is the Omnipotent Force, which is also called the Holy Ghost.[3] (The Spirit that entered Jesus was in the form of a dove (John 1.32), and the Spirit that entered His disciples was "cloven tongues like as fire" (Acts 2.3-4).

Waters: mayim, figuratively is "juice" and is also a euphemism for "semen," the fluid of life. Water is hydrogen and oxygen. Taken literally, the presence of water before the "big bang" would reinforce the idea of a "black hole" or new beginning in a continuous universe where death brings rebirth. The darkness, an aspect of which is "death," was on the surface. Spirit, the activating force, and water, the life source, represent the active and passive principles without which there is no birth or regeneration. The action of Spirit on the face of the waters would become the way of spiritual and physical birth and was the union that made possible the birth of the cosmos.

> And GOD said, Let there be light:... (Gen.
> 1.3).

---

[3] Holy: hagios (Gk), "sacred," comparable to thallo: "to warm, to foster." Ghost: pnuema (Gk), "a current of air (breath, breeze, spirit," by implication, "vital principle, mental disposition, or super human, angel."

1. And There Was Light

The burst of celestial light that manifested in the beginning was the first-born of God. This initial manifestation can be compared to the "huge fireball" of the "big bang" theory, the cosmological first-born. The problem has been explaining how the substance of life survived the initial birth pangs, because when energy is converted into matter under laboratory conditions, the equal amounts of matter and anti-matter that are produced annihilate each other as they are converted into gamma rays or high energy waves. Yet both the theory and the Bible agree that all life, which includes the substances of which we were formed, came from the "first-born."

In the Bible, the first-born, the only begotten (mono-genes), the "Son," the light, was not only the beginning of the substance of which we would be composed, but also the beginning of our consciousness. (Son applies to masculine, feminine and neuter, and also means "quality or condition.") God's first expression that manifested as light is synonymous with the Word, the Greek logos: "Something said (including the thought) also reasoning (the mental faculty) or motive":

In the beginning was the Word, and the Word was with GOD, and the Word was GOD.

The same was in the beginning with GOD.

All things were made by him;[1] and without him was not anything made that was made.

In him was life; and the life was the light of men (John 1.1-4).

---

[1] Autos (Gk.): "Self" (in the sense of automatic breath), can be masculine, feminine, or neuter, "him, her, he, she, it, one."

In essence, we are as old as the universe, and our story in this sphere begins with the appearance of the light. The evolution of the universe and the evolution of consciousness are concurrent in the Bible. Both were born of Spirit and water and both followed the same pattern of development. To understand one process is to understand both.

The light within us is personified in the Bible as the LORD (Ps. 27.1): Yehovah: "self-existence, eternal," the Omniscient Consciousness. In John 1.9, the light of the Word is called the true Light, which lights everyone that comes into the world,[2] and in The Revelation (19.11-13) the allegorical rider of the white horse, who is called Faithful and True, is named the Word of God. With the article in John 1, the Word is defined as "Divine expression (i.e. Christ)."

The Divine expression, the Christ, exists in all ages. Moses' preference for the reproach of Christ is referred to in Heb. 11.26. In the *Zohar* (Matt 51), the light in Genesis is the light of the eye, the hidden light, which was shown to the first Adam, given back to Moses on Mt. Sanai, and shown to David. Jesus called the light of the body the eye, which fills the whole body with light when it is single (Matt. 6.22).

As one with God, the Divine expression represents the Christ consciousness, the union of the Omnipresent Consciousness and the Omniscient Consciousness: the I AM, the LORD GOD (Exod. 3.14-15) and is the second part of the Trinity:

For there are three that bear record in heaven, the Father (or Parent: "pater"), the Word and the Holy Ghost: and these three are one (1 John 5.7).

The Trinity as Omnipresence, Omniscience, Omnipotence (all present, all knowing, and all powerful), can be compared to energy, mind, and force, which becomes matter, consciousness, and motion when activated.

One theory of how matter survived the conversion to produce life is based on the discovery that what were considered inviolable laws governing subatomic particles are sometimes violated. While according to the law of physics, every reaction has its mirror image - equal amounts of matter and anti-matter are produced, the theory is that the protons out-numbered the anti-protons and one proton in a billion survived to form the universe. The "happenstance" that allowed for this violation of the law of physics can be compared to the Biblical "grace," the condition that allows for the performance of "miracles" that violate

---

[2] LB reads: "lighted every man that came into the world." Both words are used as past and present tenses in the Bible. Since the light of men was manifested in the beginning and is eternal, either KJV or LB can considered to be correct.

the laws of physics, and which is an attribute of the Word (John 1.14).

Light and Darkness

In the Bible, the process of creation is not happenstance, but is orchestrated by the intelligence of the First Cause:

> And GOD saw the light, that it was good: and GOD divided between the light and between the darkness (Gen. 1.4).[3]

Light: owr, means "illumination (in every sense): including "lightning, happiness and enlightenment." To "see the light" is to become aware, to illuminate the consciousness. In Proverbs, Solomon wrote of that illumination, the primal wisdom and understanding:

> The LORD possessed[4]me [wisdom and understanding] in the beginning of his way, before his works of old.

> I was set up from everlasting, from the beginning, or ever the Earth was. When there were no depths I was brought forth: when there were no fountains abounding with water

> Before the mountains were settled, before the hills was I brought forth: While as yet he had not made the Earth, nor the field (open places), nor the highest part (beginning) of the dust of the world (Prov. 8.22-26).

Another theory on how matter and anti-matter avoided annihilating each other is that they were repelled by the mutual forces of gravity and anti-gravity. John 1 continues:

> And the light shineth in darkness: and the darkness comprehended (or seized) it not.

---

[3] KJV margin. Marginal notes are a closer rendition of the original.
[4] KJV margin.

Divided: badal, also means, "distinguish, differ and select." The light, which was "good" (or best), like the protons of the theory, was selected as the means by which the plan of creation was implemented:

> For by him [the son, the firstborn] were all
> things created that are in heaven and that are
> in Earth, visible and invisible (Col. 1.16).[5]

Since the life, the Christ consciousness, the constructive force, is the light, its opposite, the darkness, the destructive force, can be considered to be anti-life, the anti-Christ consciousness. These two forces appear in many forms in the Bible. The light is synonymous with the LORD, the Christ, the Messiah, the Savior, the Redeemer, the Lamb of God, the Alpha and Omega, the Prince of Peace, and the Son of God, whose attributes are grace and truth and who symbolizes "good." The darkness is synonymous with Satan: "an opponent, the arch enemy of good, adversary, false accuser," the anti-Christ, the dragon, the serpent, the tempter, the devil, the son of perdition and Belial, whose attributes are rebellion and deception and who symbolizes "evil."

In the story of creation in the Zend-Avesta,[6] the light and darkness are personified as Mazda and Ahriman, two sons of God. Mazda, the god of light, is the spirit of "good," who was the instrument of creation. Ahriman, the god of darkness, is the spirit of "evil," who was banished. Ahriman remains the arch rival of Mazda, but in the end the god of light will triumph over the god of darkness.

In *The Dead Sea Scriptures* (Gaster 48, 399), the light and the darkness are called the spirit of truth and the spirit of perversity, the two spirits within man that were created by a God of knowledge in the beginning. All who practice righteousness are under the domination of the

---

[5] Also see Ps. 136.2-7, 146.5-6, Acts 14.15 & 2 Pet. 3.5.

[6] There is no record of when the Zend-Avesta was written. Origin of the language in which the Zend-Avesta (or Avesta - law of - Zend, as it is called by the Parsees of India) is obscure and is alternately called Avesta and Zend. It is the holy book of law of the early Mazdian religion of the Persians (Zoroastrianism) which was the religion of the Magi. The Avesta and the Veda (Sanskrit Scriptures) are said to be from the same source, though diversely altered. There are many similarities between the Bible and the Zend-Avesta, which gives an account of the creation, the first man, the flood, the receiving of the law, the coming Messiah and the triumph of the son of light. Its religious practices include ceremonies of purification and atonement, prayers of praise, and confession of faith, and it records revelations and prophecies.

Prince of Light and all who practice perversity are under the domination of the Angel of Darkness. In the conflict, the sons of light will triumph over the sons of darkness.

Whether they are called matter and anti-matter, Christ consciousness and anti-Christ consciousness, the god of light and the god of darkness, or something else, the light and darkness represent two aspects of the universal constructive/destructive force, just as God, the First Cause, by any name is the Creative Force.

Separation of these two forces took place on the omnipresent level before the Earth as a habitation for Adamic man appeared and represented separation of matter and anti-matter and the beginning of space. While the adamic beings had not yet appeared, the division between the light and between the darkness represented the beginning of their individualized consciousness, the light beings, the Gods to whom knowledge of good and evil is ascribed in Gen. 3. 5, and of whom the Psalmist wrote:

> I have said you are Gods (Elohiym); and all of
> you are children of the Most High.

> But you shall die like men, and fall like one of
> the princes (Ps. 82.6-7).

Jesus alluded to this pre-existence as light when he prayed for that first condition of illumination:

> O Father, glorify thou me with thine own self,
> with the glory which I had with thee before the
> world was (John 17.5)

Day and Night

The distinction between the two forces is reflected in the names given them before time was established:

> And GOD called the light Day, and the darkness he[7] called Night: and the evening was, and the morning was, the first day[8] (Gen. 1.5).

---

[7] Hiy: "He, she, it, self."
[8] KJV margin.

Day: yom, "to be hot" represents a period when the consciousness is "awake," and Night: layelah, "a twist," represents a turn away from light, a period when the consciousness is obscure or "asleep." These two conditions as applied to those who follow the light are pointed out by Paul in a letter to the brethren at Thessalonica:

> You are all the children of light, and the children of day: we are not of the night, nor of darkness (1 Thess. 5.5).

Time, as we know it, does not go into effect until after the Earth appears and the two great lights are made on the "fourth day." The "first day," which began with the period of darkness and ended with the period of light, symbolized the first cycle of creation: Day (yom) also means "age." The Bible is structured around a system of numbers and their values, i.e., three represents a period of gestation on the mental/spiritual level; seven represents a spiritual cycle; ten represents a new beginning, and forty represents a period of testing. The length of this age is undeterminable, but could be either the number of the day (1) or any of these numbers increased, i.e., 1 day to 1 year, 1 thousand years, 1 million years, etc. without changing the numerological value in the way that the 40 days and nights of the flood (Gen. 7.4) were increased to 40 years in the wilderness (Num. 14.33-34). Peter's statement that "one day is with the Lord as a thousand years, and a thousand years as one day" (2 Pet. 3.8) demonstrates this and gives some idea of how time is conceived cosmically. However, as yet there was no point of reference by which to judge time as we know it.

Heaven and Earth

The overall plan of creation had been envisioned and the constructive force had been manifested. Now the process unfolded in accordance with cosmic law, which is "good." Each step was first envisioned, or called forth on the spiritual level, and then manifested:

> And GOD said, Let there be a firmament (expanse) in the midst of the waters: and let it divide the waters from the waters.

> And GOD made the firmament, and divided the waters which were under the firmament

> from the waters which were above the firma-
> ment: and it was so. And GOD called the firm-
> ament Heaven: and the evening was, and the
> morning was, the second day (Gen. 1.6-8).

Heaven, which had been created as idea in Genesis 1:1 was now made manifest. In the development of the universe and of consciousness, the waters above the firmament represented the life source on the universal level and the waters below the firmament represented the life source in this sphere. The firmament of Heaven represented the spiritual, or celestial level of consciousness and this galaxy, as the story focused on this solar system and Earth.

> And GOD said, Let the waters under the hea-
> ven be gathered together unto one place, and
> let the dry [land] [9] appear; and it was so.

> And GOD called the dry [land] Earth; and the
> gathering together of the waters called he
> Seas, and GOD saw that it was good (Gen.
> 1.9-10).

Earth, which had been created as idea in Genesis 1:1 now appeared. "Good" is the condition of the light, which is the constructive force. After God saw that the Earth was "good," THE EARTH WAS CALLED ON TO PRODUCE LIFE.

> And GOD said, Let the Earth bring forth
> grass (sprout, sprout to sprout) and the
> (grass) herb (to sow) yielding seed, and the
> fruit-tree yielding fruit after his kind, whose
> seed is in itself, upon the Earth: and it was so
> (Gen. 1.11).

The pattern of the flora was first imagined, or brought forth as idea on the spiritual level. What Gen. 1:11 literally says is: "Let the Earth sprout sprout to sprout and grass to sow." (An example of this is found in Gen. 2.5 which states that every plant was made before it was in the

---

[9] Land is an addition to the original text.

Earth and every herb before it grew.) This pattern of the flora containing seeds of reproduction can be compared to the DNA molecules of life that contain the genetic code and the hereditary information. It was so, but then Gen. 1.12 states:

> And the Earth brought forth grass, and herb yielding seed after his kind, and the tree yielding fruit, whose seed was in itself, after his kind: and GOD saw that it was good.

> And the evening was and the morning was, the third day (Gen. 1.12-13).

Celestial Bodies

While the Earth and the flora had been called "good," the firmament had not been called "good." Now a major development took place in the firmament that would be "good," and that would make the Earth habitable:

> And GOD said, Let there be lights in the firmament of the heaven, to divide between the day and between the night; and let them be for signs and for seasons, and for days and years.

> And let them be for lights in the firmament of the heaven to give light upon the Earth: and it was so (Gen. 1.14-15).

The division, or selection, between the light (Day) and between the darkness (Night) by God on the first day (or in the first age) marked the beginning of space and the Gods who knew good and evil. This division, which will come from the lights: "luminous bodies," in the firmament of heaven, will mark the beginning of time and the distinction of types of the Gods, the "Sons." In the evolution of the universe and of consciousness, the lights are the celestial bodies. The celestial bodies of the "Sons" are described in Psalm 104:

> Bless the LORD, O my soul, O LORD my

GOD, you are clothed with honor and majesty:

Who covers [yourself] with light as [with] a garment; who stretched out the heavens like a curtain:

Who lays the beams of his chambers in the waters: who makes the clouds his chariot: who walks upon the wings of the wind;

Who makes his angels (messengers) spirits: his ministers (servants) a flaming fire:

The luminous bodies were first called for on the spiritual level. Then:

GOD made two great lights; the greater light for the rule of day, the lesser light for the rule of night: [he made] the stars also.

And GOD set them in the firmament of the heaven to give light upon the Earth.

And to rule over the day, and over the night, and to divide the light from the darkness: And GOD saw that it was good.

And the evening was, and the morning was, the fourth day (Gen. 1.16-19).

The lights that were set in the firmament by God, were specifically to give light upon the Earth. (A current comparison would be the satellites set in the sky to give knowledge (enlightenment) to Earth and the proposal to place a solar satellite in the sky as an energy source.)

Though the two great lights are not identified as the sun and moon, they are accepted as such in Psalm 136.7-9, which also clarifies the role of the stars: "the sun to rule by day...the moon and stars to rule by night." A possible reason why the sun and moon are not identified could be the same reason that Elohiym is not translated as Gods: to avoid idolatry. In the land of Abraham's nativity, moon worship was practiced, and in Egypt, the land of Moses' nativity, the sun was revered. In Deuteronomy, where Moses instructed the people against idol worship, he stated:

> And lest you lift up your eyes unto heaven, and when you see the sun and the moon, and the stars, all the host heaven, should be driven to worship them, and serve them, which the LORD your GOD has divided (allotted) unto all nations under the whole heaven (Deut. 4.19).

The sun is first mentioned in Genesis 15.12 as going down as Abraham went into a deep sleep (trance). The implication here is a link between the sun and the "day" consciousness. The sun and the moon are first mentioned together as they and the eleven stars bowed down to Joseph in his dream. Here, they symbolized his father, mother, and eleven brothers according to Jacob's interpretation (Gen. 37.9-10).

In relationship to Earth, the two great lights, the sun and the moon, represent the active principle that rules the conscious forces, and the passive principle that rules the subconscious forces, and the stars represent the twelve basic patterns of activity, or forms of expression of the light that lights everyone who comes into the world (that later would be personified by Jacob's twelve sons, who would, like the Mazzaroth, also symbolize the twelve major divisions of the body).

The twelve divisions of the celestial band are called houses (the same as the tribes of Israel) and the star groups are called constellations. The constellations were given names by the ancients that describe different personality traits, i.e., Taurus, the bull, describes strength and willfulness.

The lights were made for the rule (memshalah, "realm, dominion") of the day and the night -- the two states of mind -- and to rule (mashal, "have power over") the day and night: the divisions of time. Their methods of rule, the influences that their emanations or gravitational pull exerts on Earth, varies according to their positions in the sky and the relationship to each other of the transiting planets, i.e., the moon's influence on the tides and emotions, the sun's effect on life on the Earth and changes of the seasons vary according to their orbiting positions. These influences of the moon and the sun are understood because they are evident. There are other influences that are felt, but are not as evident to the conscious mind. In the story of Job, where he is questioned about memory of his beginning, he is also questioned about his ability to rule over these influences:

> Where is the way where light dwells: and as for darkness where is the place thereof,

> That you should take it to the bound thereof, and that you should know the paths to the house thereof?

> Do you know it, because you were then born? or because the number of your days is great?

> Can you bind the sweet influences of Pleiades (the seven stars)[10] or loose the band of Orion?

> Can you bring forth Mazzaroth (the twelve signs)[11] in his season? Can you guide Arcturus with his sons?

> Do you know the ordinances of heaven? Can you set the dominion thereof in the Earth? (Job 38.19-21, 31-33).

The heavenly bodies Job were questioned about are in our galaxy, the Milky Way. The Mazzaroth is the celestial band, the Zodiac. Pleiades is a cluster of several hundred stars in the constellation Taurus, six of which are visible to the naked eyed. In mythology, Pleiades are the seven daughters of Atlas and Pleione: Maia, Electra, Celaeno, Tygeta, Merope, Alcyone and Sterope, who were metamorphosed into stars

---

[10] "The seven stars," KJV margin. Also see Amos 5.8 and Job 9.9. In mythology, Pleiades are the seven daughters of Atlas and Pleione: Maia, Electra, Celaeno, Tygeta, Merope, Alcyone and Sterope, who were metamorphosed into stars along with Orion and his dog. Electra is not seen because she is in mourning for Troy. In the Bible, on the individual level, the seven stars symbolize seven aspects of consciousness within, the seven angels (Rev. 1.20).

[11] "The twelve signs," KJV margin.

along with Orion and his dog. Electra is not seen because she is in mourning for Troy. In the Bible, on the individual level, the seven stars symbolize seven aspects of consciousness within, the seven angels (Rev. 1.20). Orion is a constellation in the celestial equator near the constellations Gemini and Taurus, and Arcturus is the brightest star in the constellation Bootes. There is no specific mention in the Bible of the formation of the planets. The only planet mentioned in the Bible is the morning star (Venus). However, mazzalah: "a constellation, Zodiac sign," is translated as planets in 2 Kings. 23.5. Star: kowkab, is best defined as a "round, rolling, shiny object." In the cosmological order, stars appear before the planets. Genesis 1.16 states only "[he made] the stars also." Whether the stars appeared before the planets or whether "stars" include the planets is open to interpretation. The main focus in the Bible is on Earth, our planet. Heaven, which has come to be regarded as the "hereafter" is made up of celestial bodies. Jesus's statement at the last supper, "in my Father's house are many mansions...I go to prepare a place for you" (John 14.2) applied to the universal level suggests that there are other realms where consciousness (not necessarily physical bodies) reside in the "Father's house."

In this solar system, nine known planets plus the sun and the moon transit the houses of the celestial band. The planets were given names of the ancient hero Gods that are associated with certain attributes. A clue to how consciousness is expressed in the other realms might possibly be in the attributes associated with the planets. For example, in Earth, "to be firm," the third planet from the Sun, which is associated with the physical, consciousness is expressed in three-dimensional matter and development in the physical is experienced.

Pluto, the ninth planet, was named after the Roman god of the dead and ruler of the underworld (the Greek Hades) and is associated with self and consciousness. On Pluto consciousness might well be in darkness or at the gestation stage, at the sub-level of "the deep."

Neptune, the eight planet was named after the Roman god of the sea (the Greek Poseidon) and is associated with the psyche and mysticism. Here consciousness might be expressed as the union of spirit and water.

Uranus, the seventh planet was named for the supreme Greek god, the "personification of heaven," and is associated with extremes and the psychic realm. It might well be the "heaven" where consciousness is expressed as light, the Gods who knew the extremes of good and evil.

Saturn, the sixth planet, was named after the Roman god (the Greek Cronus) and is associated with malevolence and change. Interestingly, Saturn's rings resemble grooves in a record and the "braided" rings look like strands of DNA. It might well be a place where consciousness is programmed or changed, "the place of judgement." It is within the realm of possibility that consciousness is expressed as the particles that make up the rings.

Jupiter, the fifth planet, was named after the supreme Roman god (the Greek Zeus, "Jove") and is associated with benevolence, strength and expansion. In this realm consciousness might be expanded and expressed as the complete circle, both polarities.

Mars, the fourth planet, was named after the Roman god of war (the Greek Ares) and is associated with madness and violence. Consciousness on Mars could possibly be expressed in the form of unbridled energy.

Venus, the second planet, was named after the Roman goddess (the Greek Aphrodite) and is associated with love and beauty. While the data received from Venus makes it appear to be a "hell" for physical man, consciousness expressed as love falls in the category of feeling or emotion, and possibly can be expressed on Venus as heat waves.

Mercury, the first planet, was named after the Roman god (the Greek Hermes), the messenger of the Gods, and is associated with mind and communication. Consciousness on Mercury could possibly be expressed as thought waves.

Living Creatures

Genesis 1.20-22 appears to hold the answer to the riddle of the evolutionary process in the creation story. After the solar system was deemed harmonious, "good," THE WATERS WERE CALLED ON TO PRODUCE ANIMAL LIFE.

> And GOD said, Let the waters bring forth
> abundantly the moving creature that has life,
> and fowl that may fly above the Earth in the
> open (face of the) firmament of heaven (Gen.
> 1.20).

When God called for and made the firmament, it was so. When God called for the Earth to appear, it was so. When God called for the pattern of the flora, it was so. And God made the lights and set them in the firmament. Here God called on the waters to produce life, but as yet it was not so. Moving creature: sherets, means "a swarm, active mass of minute animals," from sharats: "to wriggle, to breed," and can describe the first-stage microscopic life that will be brought forth from the waters.

> And GOD created great whales and every liv-
> ing creature that moves, which the waters
> brought forth abundantly after his kind, and
> every winged fowl after his kind: and GOD saw
> that it was good (Gen. 1.21).

This was God's second creation. The first was the heaven(s) and the Earth. Great whales: tanniym, means "a marine or land monster, sea serpent or jackal, dragon (as preternaturally formed)," from tan, "to elongate," and living creature: chay nephesh, means "living, breathing (creature)," as opposed to a wriggling mass. (Nephesh, which is translated as "soul" is also translated as "body.")[12]

The pattern of the steps of evolution of the moving creatures from "minute animals" to a variety of individual species, including birds and prehistoric animals, were created as idea and will evolve in harmony with nature, or cosmic order, which is "good."

> And GOD blessed them, saying, Be fruitful
> and multiply, and fill the waters in the seas,
> and let fowl multiply in the Earth. And the
> evening was, and the morning was, the fifth day
> (Gen. 1.22-23).

Multiply here is rabah: "increase (in whatever respect)." The living creatures were created as thought, but not yet manifested. The gestation period of the second creation reached term in the evolutionary process in the sixth cycle when the thought forms of the living creatures became "firm."

> And GOD said, Let the Earth bring forth the
> living creature after his kind, and creeping
> thing, and beast (life) of the Earth after his
> kind: and it was so (Gen. 1.24).

The living (breathing) creature (s) (chay nephesh), the cattle: behe-mowth, "quadrupeds," the creeping thing: remes, "reptiles" and the beast: chay, "life" of the Earth, were first envisioned from that which had been created as idea then:

---

[12] See Lev. 21.11, Num. 6.6, 9.6, 7, 10, 19.11, 13, 16 & Hag. 2.13.

> GOD made the beast (life) of the Earth after
> his kind, and the cattle after his kind, and
> every thing that creeps upon the Earth
> (ground) after his kind: and GOD saw that it
> was good (Gen. 1.25).

Order of the Biblical evolution is consistent with the order of the
theory of evolution: first plants, then marine/land life and winged creatures, then mammals. However, at this point the similarity between the
scientific and Biblical theories ends because of the same missing element in the creation theory: consciousness, which is considered to be
the end result of the scientific theory, is the beginning of Biblical creation. Biblically, God, the Omnipresent Consciousness, the First Cause
in nature, had created the heaven (s) and the Earth on the spiritual level
as a plan, then step-by-step they were manifested. Animal life had been
the second plan of creation on the spiritual level that manifested. Now,
a third plan was envisioned, not as a physical evolutionary link to the
animals, but as a joint separate creation, a spiritual extension of the
triune Consciousness.

> And GOD said, Let us make man (adam:
> mankind) in our image after our likeness; and
> let them have dominion over the fish of the
> sea, and over all the Earth, and over every
> creeping thing that creeps upon the Earth
> (Gen. 1.27).

In the Image of God
GOD is described in the Bible as Spirit (John 4.24), love (1 John
4.8), light (1 John 1.5) and invisible (Col. 1.15), but "not a man (ish:
masculine), nor the son of man (adam: mankind)" (Num. 23.19), and
the LORD, the Omniscient Consciousness, the Constructive Force, the
Son, is described as light and the image: "The image of the invisible
God, the firstborn of every creature is the Son (Col. 1.13-15)." Image:
tselem, is "to shade, phantom (fig.) illusion."

> So GOD created man in his [own] image, in
> the image of GOD created he him: male
> (zakar) and female (negebah) created he them
> (Gen. 1.27).

The proposal was to jointly "make" mankind, but first these beings were "created" by God in the image and likeness of God on the spiritual level just like the heaven and the Earth and the living creatures had first been created on the spiritual level. As reflections of God, the spiritual images, the sons (or children) of God, mirrored God, the total force, which contains both polarities: the male/female, active/passive, yin/yang principles, opposites and balance (that would be separated later). A clearer rendition of Gen. 1.27 is in Gen. 5-2: "Male and female created he them and called their name Adam (mankind)."

Spiritual mankind, the images, had been the final creation of GOD, the First Cause, then:

> GOD blessed them, and GOD said unto
> them, Be fruitful and multiply, and replenish
> the Earth, and subdue it: and have dominion
> over the fish of the sea, and over the fowl of
> the air (heaven) and over every living thing
> that moves upon the Earth (Gen. 1.28).

While God had called on the Earth to bring forth herbs and fruit trees containing seed that brought forth after its kind, and the fish and fowl had been given the injunction to multiply after their kinds, spiritual mankind, the images of God, were not given seed nor the injunction to bring forth after their kind. (Their "kind" would have been other spiritual images.) The injunction given to spiritual mankind was simply to multiply: rabah, "increase (in whatever respect)."

Replenish: "To fill or make complete again, add a new stock" has a wide application. As used here and after the flood (Gen. 9.1), replenish implies a new beginning. (The first order in spirit was in the beginning as the light that was called forth to bring order out of chaos.)

> And GOD said, Behold, I have given you
> every herb bearing (seeding) seed, which is
> upon the face of all the Earth, and every tree
> in which is the fruit of the tree yielding seed:
> to you it shall be for meat (Gen. 1.29).

The created images, as spirit like God, had no need of food as long as they were spiritual beings. The herbs and fruit of the trees here are intended for sustenance literally and figuratively of the physical beings that would be made. The animals would be herbivorous.

> And to every beast (life) of the Earth, and to
> every fowl of the air (heaven), and to every
> thing that creeps upon the Earth, wherein
> [there is] life, [I have given] every green herb
> for meat: and it was so.

> And GOD saw every thing that he had made:
> and behold, it was very good. And there was
> evening, and there was morning, the sixth day
> (Gen. 1.30-31).

At the end of the sixth cycle, the creation of the Earth as a self-sustaining planet ruled by the lights was completed and in harmony with the First Cause: it was "very good."

> Thus the heavens and the Earth were finished,
> and all the host of them. And on the seventh
> day GOD ended his work which he had made:
> and he rested on the seventh day from all his
> work which he had made. And GOD blessed
> the seventh day, and sanctified it: because that
> in it he had rested from all his work which
> GOD created and made [Or, "created to
> make"][13] (Gen. 2.1-2).

Creation was completed and that created was left to gel or evolve as GOD, the First Cause, rested. Seven is a spiritual number that corresponds to the spiritual body symbolized by the seven angels of The Revelation. Since the creation story was recorded after Moses gave the Ten Commandments, this is not a foreshadowing, but a reinforcement of the third Commandment to rest on the seventh day.

Spiritual mankind, the images of GOD, who functioned in the spiritual body, were free to multiply in whatever respect. However, physical humans able to function in the third dimension had not yet made their debut on the planet:

> there was not a man (adam) to till the ground
> Gen. 2.5).

---

[13] KJV margin.

Symbology
1. And There Was Light

GOD - The Omnipresent Consciousness, the First Cause in nature, the Infinite Mind.

SPIRIT OF GOD - The Omnipotent Consciousness, the Activating Force.

LIGHT - The Omniscient Consciousness, the Constructive Force, the First-born, the Son, the Word, the Lord, the Christ Consciousness, the Master.

DARKNESS - The rebellious force, the anti-light, the anti-Christ Consciousness.

DAY - The state of consciousness of the Light.

NIGHT - The state of unconsciousness of the Light.

WATER - The nurturing source of life on the spiritual and physical levels.

HEAVEN - The spiritual/ethereal level of consciousness.

EARTH - The physical level of consciousness, the ground of life in the physical.

TWO GREAT LIGHTS - Rulers of the two levels of consciousness, the sun and moon consciousness, mental and emotional.

THE STARS - Expressions of the Light Consciousness in the heavenly level that are reflected in the physical consciousness as basic patterns of activity.

MANKIND IN THE IMAGE OF GOD - Spiritual Sons of God, creations of the Creator, the spiritual body.

2. Let Us Make Man

T he first condition of the sons of God as divisions of consciousness in the beginning on the spiritual realm was as light. That same light, the Son, the LORD, the constructive force, was the image: the spiritual body, the created, the firstborn of every creature (Col. 1.13-15).[1]

The Sons of God

Greek and Roman "mythology" abound with the exploits of the sons of God, and they are mentioned in Genesis and Job, but only two Biblical characters are called sons of God: Adam (Luke 3.38) and Jesus (John 10.36). Melchizedek, who materialized from the celestial realm, was called "like unto the Son of God" (Heb. 7.3).[2]

As spiritual beings like the angels in the celestial realm, the sons of God, as mankind the images, could ride on the clouds and walk on the wings of the wind, but they were not functional in a three-dimensional plane (they could not "till the ground") unless they materialized.

The ability to manifest in the material realm from the celestial realm and vice versa was not only demonstrated in the Bible by Melchizedek, who materialized as the priest of the Most High God (Gen. 14.18), but by Enoch, who walked with God (i.e., was in harmony with the Omnipresent Consciousness) and dematerialized (Gen. 5.24, Heb. 11.5), and by Jesus, who did both. Also, the angels who appeared in the Bible and ate with Abraham and with Lot, and wrestled with Jacob, etc. had materialized and were alternately called men and Lords.[3]

Solomon's Proverb on the primal wisdom and understanding traced the progression from the beginning to the first forms manifested by the Sons of God, by mankind the images of light:

When he [the LORD] prepared the heavens, I

---

[1] Also see 2 Cor. 4.4.

[2] The disciples were called sons of God by faith: Gal. 3.26, 1 John 3.1-2, Rom. 8.14-16, etc.

[3] See Gen. 16.13, 18.2, 19.5, 32.24, Josh. 5.13, etc.

[was] there: when he set a compass (circle)
upon the face of the depth:

When he established the clouds above, when
he strengthened the fountains of the deep:

When he gave to the sea his decree, that the
waters should not pass his commandment;
when he appointed the foundations of the
earth:

Then I was by him, [as] one brought up [with
him] and I was daily [his] delight, rejoicing
always before him:

Rejoicing in the habitable part of his earth;
and my delights [were] with the sons of men
(Prov. 8.27-31).

The Sons of Men

A clear distinction is made in the Bible between sons of men (ben
adam)[4] and mortal men (enos).[5] However, the term continues to be con-
fusing because the sons of men: manifestations of the created images,
the spiritual man, preceded formation of the physical man. Even though
Jesus, who referred to himself as the Son of God and the Son of man,
attempted to explain this when he said the Son of man was spirit and life
(John 6.53, 63), the difference was not clearly understood by some of the
people of his time, including Nicodemus, who was a learned scholar and
master of Israel. Jesus explained to him: "That which is born of flesh is
flesh; and that which is born of Spirit is spirit" (John 3.6), and that the
Son of man came down from heaven and must be lifted up again. When
the people said to him, "We have heard out of the law that Christ abides
forever: but how sayest thou, the Son of man must be lifted up? Who is
this Son of man?" he gave them the answer in a parable:

---

[4] Ben: "son (as the builder of a family name)" also means "children, daughter,
grandson, nation, subject, etc."
[5] See Job 3.8, Ps. 90.3, 144.3 & Isa. 51.12, 52.14.

> Yet a little while is the light with you. Walk
> while you have the light, lest darkness come
> upon you: for he that walks in darkness knows
> not where he goes. While you have light,
> believe in the light, that you may be children
> of light (John 12.34-36.).

Manifestations of the created as sons of men was a step down from the GOD stage, but a step above that of mortal man. David wrote:

> What is man (enos) that you O LORD (Yeho-
> vah)[6] our LORD (Adon)[7] are mindful of him?
> and the son of man (ben adam), that you visit
> him? For you have made him a little lower
> than the GODS (Elohiym)[8] and have crowned
> him with glory and honor (Ps. 8.4-5).

Lord of the Seventh Day

The planet Earth was a playground for the sons of men (Prov. 8.27-31). The absolute dominion that they had been given over the forces of the planet is reflected in the statement made by Jesus when he had been accused of healing on the seventh day. He replied, "The Son of man is LORD even of the Sabbath-day" (Matt. 12.8).

As the sons of men exercised creativity in conjunction with wisdom and understanding, they were a source of delight. A glimpse of the heights reached by that ancient civilization is given in Daniel's vision:

> I beheld till the thrones were cast down, and
> the Ancient of days did sit, whose garment was
> white as snow, and the hair of his head like the
> pure wool: his throne was like a fiery flame,
> and his wheels as burning fire.
>
> I saw in the night visions, and behold, one like
> a son of man came with the clouds of heaven,
> and came to the Ancient of days, and they

---

6 Yehovah: "self-existence, eternal."

7 Adon: "sovereign, i.e., controller, master."

8 The original word is Elohiym: GODS, but some versions read "angels." Angel is malak.

brought him near before him (Dan. 7.9, 13).

These Ancients who came out of the clouds and whose "thrones" were propelled by flame and had wheels, exemplified a society that was highly advanced (either by means of the pure imaginative force or imagination applied to technology). Ezekiel, who went back in consciousness to his original state in Earth as a son of man (he was addressed throughout the vision as "son of man") gives a description of one of these flying machines (Ezek. 1.4-28). It came out of the clouds in a whirlwind accompanied by brightness. The design incorporated replicas of hybrid creatures, the Cherubim. It had wheels that moved when it moved, a ring around it with "eyes," an expanse the color of the "terrible crystal" around the top, and in the throne was one like the appearance of a son of man. It went straightforward and ran and returned as a flash of lightning!

The terminology used by Daniel and Ezekiel to describe these flying machines was based on their current knowledge. To Daniel it was a covered throne with wheels and to Ezekiel it was a "living creature" because it moved. Today we would use different words to describe these flying machines. At this writing we do not have a flying machine with that kind of maneuverability (though we are getting close), but according to Ecclesiastes what was in the past will be in the future:

> The thing that has been, it is that which shall be: and that which is done is that which shall be done: and there is no new thing under the sun. Is there any thing whereof it may be said, See, this is new? it has been already of old time, which was before us (Eccles. 1.9-10).

Not only the current technology may be a return cycle, but also the recombining of heredity patterns to make new life forms.

Cherubim and Nephilim

While the flora and fauna had been programmed to "bring forth after their kinds," mankind as the created image on the spiritual level had not. They had simply been blessed to multiply: rabah: "increase (in whatever respect)."

The Cherubim, who were already in existence when Adam,the physical man, was sent out of Eden (Gen. 3.24), were composite creatures. Ezekiel described these sphinx-like forms as having wings, and faces like that of a man, a bull, a lion and an eagle, and the likeness of a man (Ezek. 1.5-10) and called them "living creatures" (Ezek. 10.20).

A clue to the various other kinds of forms that the images "multiplied" is in Genesis 6.4, which states that Nephilim[9] were in the earth when mankind (adam) began to multiply (rabab: "increase by the myriad") on the face of the earth (ground) and also after that.

Nephilim: from naphal, "to fall" and nephal, "untimely birth," is an apt description of the first attempts to establish the perfect form for human beings. The varied composite forms of the descendants of the Nephilim are described by their names: sons of Seir ("satyr"), Anakim, sons of Arba ("quardrate") Zuzim ("full-breasted, wild beasts") Emim ("bugbears, terrors") Rephaim ("giants") and Horim ("troglodyte"). Josephus, the first-century historian, wrote of the Nephilim still in existence during Abraham's time:

> There were till then left the race of giants, who had bodies so large, and countenances *so entirely different from other men*, that they were surprising to the sight and terrible to the hearing. The bones of these men are still shown to this very day, *unlike to any credible relations to other men* (Josephus 110) [Italics mine].

In *The Natural History*, Pliny (80) describes a variety of composite beings: satyrs, gorgons, cyclops, mermaids, etc. and said that he had seen the embalmed remains of a Hippocentaur (half man, half horse). Ezekiel also said the paramours of ancient Egypt had flesh like that of asses and issue like that of horses (Ezek 23. 20). Replicas of the composite beings appear in the art of the ancient world, especially that of the Egyptians and Assyrians, but except for the visuals mentioned by Pliny, there appears to be no record of the discovery of composite beings. It is possible that fossils like the female Neanderthal skull and bones of an Ibex that were found together in a cave on Gibraltar (Gore 30, 34-35) could belong to the same skeleton, but have not been recognized as such because centaurs, satyrs, harpies, and cherubim, etc. are thought to have been mythological creatures. However, fossils of "giants" eight feet tall have been discovered in the United States and in Mexico (Steiger 20).

---

[9] NAB, MT and NEB list the original word, "Nephilim." LB, KJV and GNB list a translation, "giants."

The Ammonites called the descendants of the Nephilim, Zamzummim, "intriguing, to imagine." The hybrid Cherubim are rightly defined as imaginary, but Ezekiel also called them "living creatures" (chay: alive). And he received a message by the word of the Lord that the king of Tyrus had been the anointed Cherub in Eden (Ezek. 28.12-15).

Paul's statements to the Romans when speaking of invisible things from the creation of the world is an apt description of the "living creatures":

> Because that which may be known of God, is manifest in them (the just); for God has shown [it] unto them.
>
> For the invisible things of him from the creation of the world are clearly seen, being understood by the things that are made, [even] his eternal power and Godhead; so that they are (or may be) without excuse:
>
> Because that when they knew God, they glorified [him] not as God, neither were thankful, but became vain in their IMAGINATIONS, and their foolish heart[10] was darkened. Professing themselves to be wise, they became fools,
>
> And changed the glory of the uncorruptible God into an image like corruptible man, and birds, and four-footed beasts, and creeping things (Rom. 1:19-23).

In light of the advancements in genetics since the time of Paul, these passages can be viewed in another context. Currently, we know that any combination of life imaginable -- even inter-species -- is possible through genetic engineering by recombining the DNA code. All manner of genes, including some from humans, animals, and plants, have been transplanted into bacteria. Human genes have been put into living cells of plants, a gene for a bean protein has been transplanted in

---

[10] Kardia (Gk.): "the heart, i.e. (fig.) the thought or feelings (mind)."

the egg cell of a toad, and human genes have been transplanted into embryonic mouse cells. In some cases the foreign genes have been passed on from one generation to the next becoming hereditary. Human genes have been fabricated and their synthetic messages of heredity have functioned in living bacterial cells. Among the inter-species cross is that between a firefly and a tobacco plant.

Eventually, the Nephilim, whose forms were not ideal for the development of Earth beings, would become victims of natural selection. The children of Israel would be forbidden to mix with their descendants, and they would finally disappear.

Fall of the Sons of Men

Earth is a causation planet, and that which is of the Earth is earthy (1 Cor. 15.48). As the sons identified more closely with their materialized forms, they began to lose attunement with the First Cause. A description of this is in Paul's letter to the Romans:

> For the creature was made subject to vanity,
> not willing, but by reason of him (or self) who
> had subjected the same in hope[11] (Rom. 8.20).

As they became subject to the laws of the planet, they began to express physical desires. Paul's statement on the invisible things from the creation of the world continues:

> Wherefore GOD gave them up to uncleanness, through the lusts of their own hearts, to dishonor their own bodies between themselves.
>
> Who changed the truth of GOD into a lie,[12] and worshipped the creature more than the Creator, who is blessed forever (Rom. 1.24-25).

The sons who entered the earth plane and lost their attunement eventually became imprisoned in the physical, trapped in their material-

---

[11] Elipis (Gk.) "To anticipate, usually with pleasure."

[12] Truth is associated with the light and lies with the darkness.

ized forms and locked into the earth cycle. Their fall into matter is described by Jude:

> And the angels which kept not their first
> estate, but left their own habitation, he has
> reserved in everlasting chains under darkness
> unto the judgment of the great day (Jude 6).

The predicament of the sons of men who became equated with the beasts they were meant to subdue was glimpsed by the author of Ecclesiastes:

> That which has been is now: and that which is
> to be has already been; and God requires that
> which is past.

> And moreover I saw under the sun the place
> of judgment, that wickedness was there; and
> the place of righteousness, that iniquity was
> there.

> I said in my heart concerning the estate of the
> sons of men, that God might manifest them,
> and that they might see that they themselves
> are beasts (Eccles. 3.15-16, 18).

Since the Lord is not willing that any should perish, but that all should come to repentance (2 Pet. 2.9), manifesting an ideal form in which the sons could evolve became the way of salvation. The cycles of the past, present and future being the same, the situation of the sons is summed up in Romans 8.19:

> For the earnest expectation of the creature
> waiteth for the manifestation of the sons of
> God.

The high civilization of the sons of men would eventually crumble and they would fade into the mythologies of the world cultures. However, their impact would be felt on man for centuries: The early Egyptians would pay homage to stones, trees and living creatures in which they assumed they had once lived (Budge xiii). Composite forms of the sons of men would be worshipped as Gods, even by the children of Israel who were chosen to preserve the belief in the Living God. Confusion between these gods and the Parent God would give rise to various religions and the belief in transmigration of the soul, which still prevails in some cultures.

Advent of Man, the Ideal Form

Not all of the sons of God immediately fell into darkness or became entangled in matter and equated with the beasts. Those who were led by the Spirit of God were still called the Sons of God.[13]

Advent of the ideal form of the first Adam, the Son of God, was the same kind of cosmic event as the birth of Jesus, the last Adam.[14] It is described in the Lord's questioning of Job:

> Where were you when I laid the foundations
> of the earth? declare, if you have understand-
> ing.
>
> Who laid the measures thereof, if you know?
> or who stretched the line upon it?
>
> Whereupon are the foundations thereof fas-
> tened? or who laid the corner stone thereof;
>
> When the morning stars sang together, and all
> the sons of God shouted for joy? (Job 38.4-7).

When the sons of God came together for the advent of the ideal form of man, the earth had already been populated for millions of years. (Australopithecus is dated as far back as 3.7 million years ago, 3 million years before Homo sapiens.) The new situation in the heavens characterized by the harmonious influences of the morning stars, indicated a change for the better in Earth, which was somehow connected to the morning stars.

The morning stars are any planets seen in the east in the morning,

---

[13] Definition from Rom. 8.14.
[14] Jesus. See Luke 13.4 & 1 Cor. 15.43.

but only Venus, the most brilliant object in the sky after the sun and the moon, is called, "the morning star." When seen in the east before sunrise, Venus is called Phosphorous (the morning star) and when it is seen in the west after sunset it is called Hesperus (the evening star). The dual identity of this planet is symbolic of light, its Day side, and darkness, its Night side.

Mystery has always veiled the planet Venus. Now that it has revealed some of its secrets to science, it is even more mysterious. Venus is thought to contain an excess of the primordial gas argon-36 in its atmosphere, much more than Earth, which should have been more dissipated if Venus and Earth are the same age. When Earth and Venus are in conjunction, the same hemisphere of Venus always faces Earth! This suggests that the rotation of Venus is somehow locked into Earth's.

The symbolic connection between Venus and Earth is duality. Venus symbolizes love, the flip side of which is hate. On the spiritual level, love is accompanied by selflessness. On the physical level love is accompanied by possessiveness or jealousy. In The Revelation, Jesus, who is associated with love and "good," called himself "the bright and morning star" (Rev. 22.16). Another name for Venus is Lucifer: heyel, "The morning star," (which fell - Isa. 14.12) and it is often associated with Satan, the adversary, "evil." Since the sons of men had polarized into the extremes of good and evil, preparations had been made by the sons of God for a new beginning. The balance of harmony between the morning stars was the setting for the entrance of the ideal form.

The Ideal Form - Homo sapiens

Ever since the 19th Century, based on a hypothesis put forth by Julius Wellhausen (1844-1918), a German, Protestant theologian, Chapter Two of Genesis has been explained away by some as being the "second story of creation" from a so-called Yahwist (J) source, while Chapter One is attributed to a Priestly (P) source, mainly because of the sudden switch to the LORD GOD who appeared while GOD rested. However, this explanation, which is applied to the entire Old Testament by many wherever LORD or LORD GOD appears (even in the middle of a sentence where GOD also appears), does not explain the appearance of GOD, LORD, and LORD GOD in the New Testament. Computer analysis of Genesis by Yehuda T. Radday, professor emeritus of biblical studies at the Technion, Israel's institute of technology in Haifa, in a five-year linguistic analysis of the book's 20,000 words supports the belief that the work was written by one author and contradicts

Wellhausen's hypothesis (*New York Times* 11/8/81).

At first glance, Chapter Two appears to be a repeat of part of Chapter One, but when carefully examined, it is found to be entirely different. In Chapter Two everything is "made" from that which had been "created."

While the image of mankind had been *created* by GOD, the First Cause, the form was *made* by the LORD GOD, the firstborn, who as yet was still in tune with the Omnipresent Consciousness:

> Know you that the LORD he [is] (our)[15]
> GOD: [it is] he [that] has made us, and not we
> ourselves (or, and his we are):[16][we are] his
> people, and the sheep of his pasture (Ps.
> 100.3).[17]

The same pattern used on the macrocosmic level by GOD, the First Cause, in the creation of the heaven and the earth was used by the LORD GOD, the attuned consciousness, on the microcosmic level in making the ideal form of the physical man - only the pattern was reversed. Where GOD began with the heavens, the LORD GOD began with the earth:

> These are generations of the heavens and of
> the earth when they were created, in the day
> that the LORD GOD made the earth and the
> heavens (Gen. 2.4).

The symbols established in Genesis are consistent throughout the Bible, i.e., heaven symbolizes the spiritual realm and up, and the earth symbolizes the physical realm and down, etc. The ideal body for mankind that will be formed will be descended from the heavens and the earth, and will be both physical and spiritual, but the physical body will precede the spiritual body.

The pattern of the physical being was first formed as thought:

> And every plant of the field before it was in

---

[15] LB reads "our God," which appears to be a clearer rendition since it does not confuse the firstborn with the First Cause.

[16] KJV margin.

[17] Also see Ps. 119.73.

the earth, and every herb of the field before it
grew: for the LORD GOD had not caused it
to rain upon the earth, and there was not a
man (adam) to till the ground (Gen. 2.5).

The earth had already brought forth the flora. Plant here is siyach:
"a shoot (as if uttered)," from siyach: "to ponder, converse (with oneself), meditate."[18] The plants represented the thought formations, in the
image created by GOD in Chapter One, before they were "firm" (in the
earth). Jesus compared people to plants when he said of those in darkness, "Every plant which my heavenly Father has not planted shall be
rooted up" (Matt. 15.13).[19] Herbs that had been given to the created
images "for meat" represented the sustaining forces within. Herb here:
eseb, "to glisten (or be green)," has a dual meaning.

But there went up a mist from the earth, and
watered the whole face of the ground (Gen.
2.6).

There are eight different words translated as ground. Here ground
is adamah: "redness," from adam: "to show blood (in the face, i.e., flush
or turn rosy) red." Man: adam, "ruddy, i.e., human being (an individual
or the species, mankind)," is also from adam: "to show blood." The
ground is the face, or surface of the earth, but here it is the whole face
(as the part that turns) of the ground (adamah) that is watered by the
mist.

And the LORD GOD formed man (adam) [of
the] dust of the ground, and breathed into his
nostrils the breath of life; and man (adam)
became a living soul (or living breathing creature: chay nephesh) (Gen. 2.7).

Dust: aphar "(as powdered or gray); hence clay, ashes, earth,"
minute particles not anchored to the earth that can be dispersed by the
wind, represented the molecular construction of a "loosely-knit" body.
A method of bringing together the molecules to form a body was

---

[18] Compare siyach: "meditate" Ps. 19.15, 23, 48, 78, 148, and siyach: "meditation"
Ps. 104.34.
[19] Also see John 15.2. 21 See 2 Cor. 4.16.

employed by Melchizedek who was "like unto a son of God" and materialized a body, and by Jesus after the crucifixion. In one instance Jesus "energized" in a closed room and invited Thomas to touch him (John 20.26-27), and in another he ate fish and honey while in the re-materialized body (Luke 24:13). The mist represented the water, the source of life, the hormones.

While the animals were created and made chay nephesh: living breathing creatures, "living souls," with no special action by GOD to make them animate, here a special action was taken with man formed from the dust of the ground by the LORD GOD. Breath here is nesh-ama, "puff, wind, i.e., vital breath, divine inspiration, intellect," and is also translated as soul and as spirit. The original state of the created images was as spirit, the spiritual body. John describes the trinity in the physical as spirit, water and blood:

> There are three that bear witness in the earth,
> the spirit, the water, and the blood: and these
> agree in one (1 John 5.8).

The physical trinity was completed when the LORD GOD, the attuned state of the son, the spiritual body, breathed into his nostrils the breath of life and man became a "living soul." Prior to the first inde-pendent breath, the body formed was not animate, it was not a "living soul." (Which answers the age-old question of when the soul enters the body, when human life begins.) When the spirit, the spiritual body, the image, the Son, the Lord, became the inner being, merging adam, the created image, the spiritual body, with adam, the ideal physical form, Adam, the physical human race began.

Symbology
2. Let Us Make Man

SONS OF MEN - Creations of the created, thought form manifestations of the Sons of God.

LORD GOD - The Omniscient Consciousness in attunement with the Omnipresent Consciousness, the I AM.

LORD - The Omniscient Consciousness, the Son, the image of God within, the I, the ego, the soul, the spiritual body.

HEAVEN - The spiritual level of consciousness in the body.

EARTH - Ground of life in the physical, and the physical level of consciousness in the body.

HERBS - Sustaining and healing forces within.

PLANTS - Thought formations that manifest as actions.

WATER - Chemical elements of which the physical body is formed.

GROUND - Elements found in Earth

MIST - The water, the source of life, the hormones.

DUST - Molecular construction.

MAN (formed from the dust of the ground by the LORD GOD - The Ideal physical form for Homo sapiens made by the LORD, the image, in attunement with GOD, the Creator.

BREATH OF LIFE - Vital breath, intelligent activating spirit.

MAN A LIVING SOUL - Homo sapiens containing the inner spiritual body the image of God, the Son of God.

3. The Garden of Eden

 The human being's first abode was not made by physical labor, but by use of the god-like abilities of the inner attuned consciousness, the LORD GOD:

> And the LORD GOD planted a garden east-
> ward in Eden; and there he put the man
> (adam) whom he had formed (Gen. 2.8).

In this first reference to Eden (Gen. 2.8) the LORD GOD put the man that had been formed in the garden before it was productive. In the second reference to Eden (Gen. 2.10) a river went out of Eden to water the garden and parted into four heads. In the third reference to Eden (Gen. 2.15) the LORD GOD took the man and put him into the garden to dress and care for it. Man is put in the garden twice, once "in" and once "into."

Looking at the Bible on three levels, we get:

1) Eden of the world, somewhere in the west, is the original estate, the origin of the adamic race from which four streams of consciousness (the four heads of the river) are projected,

2) the garden eastward in Eden that applies to the individual inner man, and

3) the garden of Eden that literally applies to the abode of the patriarch Adam.

Eden: "pleasure, delight," literally and figuratively was the first estate of the adamic being. The garden eastward in Eden has become a euphemism for a fertile area (Ezke. 36.35, Joel 2.3). In Sumerian eden means "fertile plain." (Abraham, the "father" of Israel, came from Ur, which was a Sumerian city. The word could have been adopted into his

46

language.) Also, in Gen. 13.10, the plain of Jordan, which was well-watered, was compared to the garden of the LORD. Garden here is gan: "garden (as fenced)" from ganan: "to hedge about, protect: defend," and eastward here is qedmah: "the front (or as time -- before, antiquity, anciently)" from qadmah: "to project (oneself)." In Job (31.33) the place where Adam hid his iniquity (from the presence of the LORD GOD among the trees of the garden) is compared to the bosom. The garden symbolizes an inner fertile place, the inner "paradise," the kingdom of GOD, which is within.[1]

> And out of the ground made the LORD GOD
> to grow every tree that is pleasant to the sight,
> and good for food: the tree of life also in the
> midst of the garden, and the tree of the know-
> ledge of good and evil (Gen. 2.9).

One of the promises in The Revelation (2.7) is: "To him that overcomes will I give to eat of the tree of life which is in the midst of the Paradise of GOD." Later in The Revelation (22.2), after the symbolic process of overcoming (regeneration) is completed, the tree of life is described as being in the midst of the street (of the Holy City -- the new Jerusalem, i.e., the new state of consciousness)[2] and on either side of the river of waters of life. This tree bares twelve manner of fruit, which it yields every month, and leaves that are for healing of the nations (people).

In the original state of perfection (before the fall and after regeneration) the adamic beings were under control of, and in contact with, the LORD GOD, the attuned consciousness, the wisdom and understanding displayed by the autonomic nervous system. Wisdom and understanding, and righteousness are equated with the tree of life:

> Length of days is in her [wisdom and under-
> standing] right hand: and in her left hand
> riches and honor.

> Her ways are ways of pleasantness and all her
> paths are peace.

---

[1] See Luke 17.21. Also see 1 Cor. 3.16 & 2 Cor. 6.16.
[2] Also see Gal. 4:26 & Heb. 12.22.

She is a tree of life to them that lay hold upon her (Prov. 3.16-18).

The fruit of righteous is a tree of life; (Prov. 11.30).

A wholesome tongue is a tree of life; but perverseness therein is a breach of the spirit (Prov. 15.4).

[A righteous man is] like a tree planted by the rivers of water, that brings forth his fruit in his season: his leaf also shall not wither: and whatsoever he does shall prosper (Ps. 1).

The trees made to grow out of the ground by the LORD GOD represent the purposes and functions of the inner man. The tree of life symbolizes wisdom and understanding of the unified consciousness. The tree of the knowledge of good and evil symbolizes the constructive and destructive forces in nature that were previously known by the inner man. In the body, the purposes are translated as nerve impulses (Nadis) of the spinal cord and the ganglia on either side of the spinal column, the alternating currents: Ida on the left, which terminates in the right nostril (sun breath), and Pingala on the right, which terminates in the left nostril (moon breath). (This is later symbolized as the three crosses at the crucifixion: Jesus in the center, one thief on the right, and one on the left.)

The river of the waters of life represents the flow of the purposes and the cerebrospinal fluid (later symbolized as the Jordan River), and the twelve manner of fruit represents the twelve basic patterns of action, the activities of the twelve pairs of cranial nerves[3] (See fig. 1), later symbolized as the twelve sons of Jacob and the twelve disciples. Plants, branches and trees are also euphemisms for people. Ezekiel wrote of the Assyrian:

Behold, the Assyrian [was] a cedar in Lebanon

---

[3] Olfactory, Optic, Oculomotor, Trochlear, Trigeminal (Trifacial), Abducent, Facial, Acoustic (Auditory), Glossopharyngeal, Vagus (Pneumograstric), Spinal Accessory & Hypoglossal.

Fig. 1 Base of Brain Showing 12 Pair of Cranial Nerves

CEREBRUM
Maintains conscious activity, memory, judgment, etc.

PITUITARY GLAND
Directs growth and controls activity of most glands.

1 - OLFACTORY TRACT
Carries impulses of smell from the nose.

2 - OPTIC TRACT
Carries impulses of sight from retina of the eye.

3-OCULOMOTOR NERVE
Moves muscles of eyeball; adjusts focus of lense and size of pupil; raises upper eyelid.

4 - TROCHLEAR NERVE
(Smallest cranial nerve)
Moves muscles which turn eyeball upward.

5 - TRI-GEMINAL NERVE
Carries impulses from skin of head and face, part of neck, tongue, teeth, linning of mouth, nose and surface of eyes.

6 - ABDUCENS NERVE
Moves remaining muscles of the eyeball.

7 - FACIAL NERVE
Carries impulse of taste from front of tongue, moves muscles in smiling, whistling & crying.

8 - AUDITORY NERVE
Carries impulse of sound from ear, also controls sense balance.

9-GLOSSOPHARYNGEAL NERVE
Carries impulse of taste from back of tongue.

10 - VARGUS NERVE
Most vital to life. Carries impulses from stomach, heart, large arteries, lungs & throat; moves muscles of swallowing and voice production; accelerates stomach and intestines; controls digestive glands and breath; inhibits heartbeat.

11 - ACCESSORY NERVE
(Only cranial nerve to muscles beyond head region) Moves muscles of neck & shoulders.

12 - HYPOGLOSSUS NERVE
Moves muscles of the tongue.

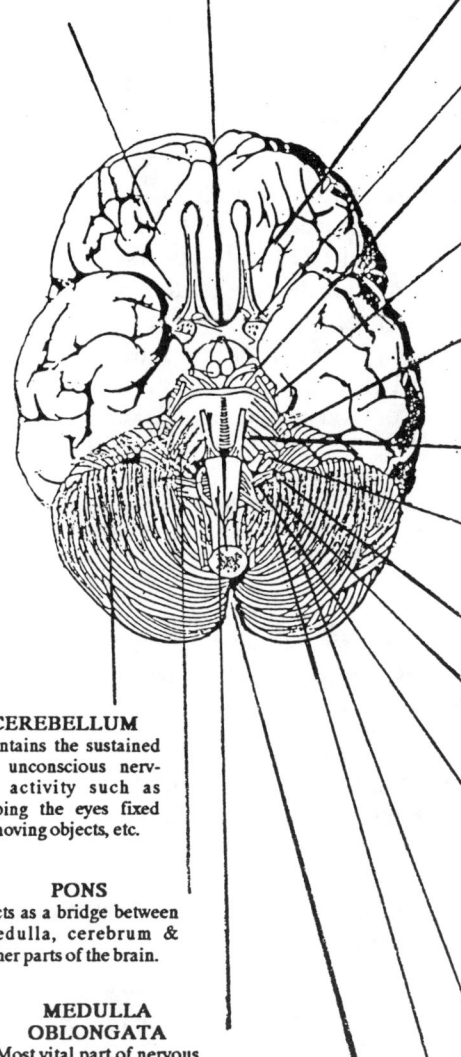

CEREBELLUM
Maintains the sustained and unconscious nervous activity such as keeping the eyes fixed on moving objects, etc.

PONS
Acts as a bridge between medulla, cerebrum & other parts of the brain.

MEDULLA OBLONGATA
Most vital part of nervous system. Maintains breath-ing and blood pressure, connects cranial nerves with all other structures of the brain.

SPINAL CORD
Carries out local reflex activities; conducts impulses to and from the brain.

> with fair branches, and with a shadowing
> shroud (forest) and of a high stature; and his
> top was among the thick boughs.

> The waters made him great, the deep set him
> up on high with her rivers running round
> about his plants, and sent out her little rivers
> unto all the trees of the field.

> The cedars in the garden of God could not
> hide him. the fir trees were not like his
> boughs, and the chestnut trees were not like
> his branches; not any tree in the garden of
> God was like unto him in his beauty.I have
> made him fair by the multitude of his
> branches; so that all the trees of Eden, that
> [were] in the garden of God envied him (Ezke.
> 31.3-4, 8-9).

The trees (the nations, the people) were all made to grow out of the adamah.

The Five Expressions

Every tree that grew out of the ground (adamah), the substance of which the first form was made, also represented the divisions of the adamic race collectively in the earth.

> And a river went out of Eden to water the gar-
> den: and from thence it was parted, and
> became into four heads (Gen. 2.10).

The river, which represented the source of consciousness in the earth, is referred to allegorically by the Psalmist:

> There is a river, the streams whereof shall
> make glad the city of God, the holy place of
> the tabernacles of the Most High (Ps. 46.4).

Tabernacle symbolizes the body temple (2 Pet. 1.13) and the dwelling place of the Living God (the Son, Lord) within:

> ...you are the temple of the living God (2 Cor.
> 1.16).

> Know you not that you are the temple of God,
> and that the Spirit of God dwells in you?

> ...the temple of God is holy, which temple you
> are (1 Cor. 3.16-17).

> For we know that if our earthly house of this
> tabernacle were dissolved, we have a building
> of God, an house not made with hands, eter-
> nal in the heavens (2 Cor. 5.1).

In Psalm 46, tabernacle is pluralized indicating more than one body, or dwelling place of the Most High. Parted here is parad: "to break through, i.e., spread or separate (oneself), sever self,"[4] and head: rosh, which has a wide application is also rendered as "a chief place, man, priest or ruler, and beginning." While the river in Eden represented the source of consciousness (the first-born) the four heads represented four other expressions of consciousness in the world and in the body.

Form of expression in the physical is through the five senses. The river and the four streams each symbolized one of the five senses and the consciousness of the five primal divisions of the adamic race. The first-born, the "only begotten" (monogenes), the LORD of LORDS,[5] as the image of GOD, was the first son of God to appear as the ideal form of the original adamic being. The four other expressions of conscious-ness can be considered spiritual clones of the first-born, who is "the true Light which lights every man that comes into the world" (John 1.9).

> (The LORD GOD) has made of one blood all
> nations of men for to dwell on the face of the

---

[4] Compare para: "(bones) out of joint," Ps. 22:14.

[5] Greek equivalent of Yehovah, Kurios of Kurios: "supreme in authority," as in Rev. 17.14 & 19.16, not as in Mark 6.21 (Megastanes: "great men"). Also see Kurios, I Cor. 8.5.

earth, and has determined the times before
appointed, and the bounds of their habitation
(Acts 17.26).

While all of humankind originally made from the adamah is of one
blood, divisions of the adamic race developed physically according to
their environments, their habitations: the yellow in Asia, the black in
Africa, etc.

Symbolically, the heads of the river represented the divisions of the
race as streams of consciousness: expressions of the senses collectively
in the world and individually in the body. Literally, they represent habitations of the descendents of the patriarch Adam in antiquity (eastward
in the garden).

The senses associated with the head are hearing, tasting, seeing and
smelling. The other physical sense, touch, is associated with the hand,
but is experienced by the entire body.

Names of some of the rivers that went out of Eden are obscure, as is
the geography.

The name of the first is Pison; that is it which
compasseth the whole land of Havilah, where
there is gold.

And the gold of that land is good: there is
bdellium and onxy stone[6] (Gen. 2.11-12).

Location of Pison ("dispersive") is obscure, and the identity of this
particular Havilah ("circular, or sandy") is uncertain. Bdellium, a gum
resin similar to true myrrh is chiefly found in western Asia and India.
Pison is thought to be the Indus, which rises out of China (southwest
Tibet) and flows through Pakistan to the Arabian Sea, but it sounds
more like a symbol for the Yellow River (Hwang Ho) of China, which
rises in the highlands of Tibet and flows 2,900 miles north, east, south
and northwest (circular) to the Gulf of Po Hai. (The Yellow River is so
named because of the yellow soil (adamah) it carries.)

Gold, being "good," is seen as an harmonious influence in the body
of the adamic being. The sense organs associated with harmony and
balance of the body are the ears. Gold: zahab, also means, "something
gold color, i.e., yellow." As a symbol of one of the senses, the first river

---

[6] Some sources read lapis lazuli, carnelian and pearls.

represents the sense of hearing. Individually in the body, the flow of this river symbolizes the cerumen, the yellowish waxy secretion of the external ear.

> And the name of the second river is Gihon:
> the same is it that compasseth the whole land
> of Ethiopia [Kuwsh] (Gen. 2.13).

Gihon: Gichown ("stream") and gachown ("belly, as the source of the fetus"), are both from goach: "to gush forth." Gihon was also the name of a spring outside of Jerusalem, the site where Solomon was proclaimed king. The biblical Ethiopia is placed in the region of the upper Nile south of the First Cataract (located in the area of Aswam), the modern southern Egypt and northern Sudan (the ancient Nubia), which did not extend as far as south as the modern Abyssinia (Hartman 386). Ethiopia means: "burnt or swarthy faced men." The name given Egypt by its ancient inhabitants, k.m.t., means "the black," and the name given the Sudan is Bilad-es-Sudan, "country of the blacks." In Gen. 13.10, Egypt is another place compared to the garden of the Lord. Gihon, as the river of Ethiopia, would symbolize the Nile, the longest river in the world. Center of the land mass of earth is located in the Nile valley, which makes it the navel of the world. The center of the body is the navel in the belly. In the physical body, this river symbolizes the intestines and the belly, which are associated with the appetites and the fetus. As one of the senses, Gihon represents the sense of taste. The feature in the head associated with taste is the mouth (or lips). Individually in the body, the flow of the second river symbolizes the saliva and digestive juices.

> And the name of the third river is Hiddekel:
> that is it which goes toward the east of (or
> front, forward part, or eastward to) Assyria.
> And the fourth river is Euphrates (Gen. 2.14).

Hiddekel, which is rendered as Tigris in the Masoretic Text, rises in the Taurus Mountains of Turkey and flows about 1,150 miles southeast where it joins the Euphrates in southern Iraq to form the Shatt-al-Arab. The Assyrian was described by Ezekiel as a tree in Eden in the garden of God and as a cedar in Lebanon: "white (mountain)." The other mention of Hiddekel is as the great river that Daniel was beside when he lifted up his eyes and saw a vision (Dan. 10.4-21). As one of the five senses in the body, this third river symbolizes the sense of sight. Individually in the body, the flow of this river symbolizes the saline liquid that is secreted by the lachrymal gland of the eye (tears). The Euphrates rises from two sources in the Armenian mountains that flow west for about 200 miles then join and flows south past northern Syria through Iraq where it joins the Tigris and flows into the Persian Gulf. In the first century A. D. Pliny wrote that the Euphrates originally had its own mouth (Enc. Brit. 816). In the symbolic book of The Revelation (9.14-15), four angels bound in the Euphrates are freed when the sixth trumpet sounds. The four angels that stand in the corners of the earth holding the four winds before the sixth trumpet sounds represent the spiritual, mental, emotional and physical aspects of man that are bound in the earth by the breath. When the man was formed, the LORD GOD breathed into his nostrils the breath of life (Gen. 2.7). The other sense associated with the head is the sense of smell, a sense experienced through the inhalation of the breath, which is the beginning of consciousness in the physical. Symbolically, this river represents the sense of smell, and by extension discernment. The feature in the head associated with the sense of smell is the nose. Individually in the body, the flow of this river symbolizes the mucin produced by the mucous membranes.

Coupled with the Tigris in Genesis 2.14, and later arising from two sources, the Euphrates ("good to cross over"), which is Perath: "to break forth, rushing" appears to have a dual symbolic meaning relating to the senses. The indication is that a division of the race utilizing perception and breath would arise in that area. However, this does not necessarily fall into the category of prophecy because it was known that Abraham, who received a call to form a particular and distinct people, crossed over from that area.

The fact that Genesis is recorded from the perspective of hind sight subject to knowledge of the compilers and is a family history on the literal level can also account for no direct identification of North and South America or the Pacific (which were not known by those names in antiquity).

In his Epistles, St. Clement, the third successor to Peter and Bishop of Rome in the First Century, A.D. wrote of worlds governed by the great master that were beyond the impassable ocean (*The Lost Books of the Bible* 122).

Site of the river that went out of Eden to water the garden in the east, is obscure. In his prophecy to Tyrus, Ezekiel compared the impending fall of that land to a place in the midst of the sea to destruction of an ancient land that sank:

When I shall bring you down with them that
descended into the pit with the people of old
time, and shall set you in the low parts of the
earth, in places desolate of old, with them that
go down to the pit, that you be not inhabited...

that you shall be no more: though you be
sought for, yet shall you never be found again,
said the Lord God (Ezke. 26.20-21).

An account of a once great civilization founded by "gods," that
flourished in antiquity is given by Plato (c. 427-347 B.C.) in his *Timaeus*.
The story of this land of Atlantis was given to Solon (c. 638-558 B.C.),
the Athenian law giver, by an Egyptian priest. Existence of this continent that vanished into the sea has been speculated upon ever since
Plato made public Solon's account. Mostly it is thought to have occu-
pied the area of the Atlantic Ocean and the eastern seaboard of N.
America.

Since catastrophic land changes occurred later, at this time the land
mass was closer together than it is now. Map of the antediluvian world
was quite different from what it is today. Frozen mastodon discovered in
Russia were found to contain undigested tropical vegetation, which
appears to confirm a pole shift that took place some time in antiquity.
In his *Histories*, Herodotus (158) gave an account related to him by the
Egyptians and their priests that in 341 generations (which he estimated
to be 11,340 years by assigning three generations to 100 years),[7] the sun
changed its usual position four times. The land that lies in the east now
was not necessarily in that position in antiquity. Discovery in the Sahara
of fish bones, including those of whales, places the Sahara underwater in
antiquity and confirms Herodotus' account that during the reign of the
first king, the land, except for the district around Thebes, was under
water and that they expanded south when it became habitable (Herodotus 104), which means that in antiquity the Nile emptied into the Atlantic.

Though Eden symbolically represented the original estate of consciousness that is now lost, the Eden of the world located somewhere
west of the garden is theorized to have been located in many places,
including Atlantis, the lost continent in the Atlantic.

---

[7] In Genesis 15.13-16 a generation is reckoned as 100 years. By this estimation 341
generations would be 34,100 years.

As the source of the four heads, the four streams of consciousness that were projected into the garden, the river of Eden symbolized the sense of touch (feelings and emotions) that is felt by the entire body. While the site of the source river is not identified, the ideal form of mankind: adam, "ruddy, red," who was formed from the adamah: "soil, from its general redness," suggests that the original source was in the red land. Individually in the body, the flow of the river of Eden symbolizes perspiration from the sweat glands.

The five divisions of the race in the earth (yellow, black, white, brown and red) and the five senses in the body (hearing, tasting, seeing, smelling and feeling) are the forms of expression of the LORD as human beings. Each division contributes a necessary element for the complete physical man in the Earth. When one sense or division of the race is affected, the whole body of the race is affected. If the expression of hearing is affected, balance and understanding of the race is impaired. If the expression of taste is affected, flavor and force of preservation of the race is diminished. If the expression of sight is affected, perception of the race is blurred. If the expression of smell is affected, detection is limited. And, if the expression of touch is affected, feeling and conscience of the total body is in jeopardy. If this expression is lost, contact with the physical is lost and the body ceases to exist either figuratively or literally, individually or collectively. Paul wrote of the necessity of all five expressions:

> For as the body is one, and has many members, and all the members of that one body, being many, are one body: so also [is] Christ...

> For the body is not one member, but many.

> If the foot shall say, Because I am not the hand, I am not the body. is it therefore not of the body?

> And if the ear shall say, Because I am not the eye, I am not of the body; is it therefore not of the body?

> If the whole body [were] an eye, where [were] the hearing? If the whole [were] hearing,

where [were] the smelling?

But now has God set the members every one of them in the body, as it has pleased him.

And if they were all one member, where [were] the body?

And the eye cannot say unto the hand, I have no need of you: nor again the head to the feet, I have no need of you.

No, much more those members of the body, which seem to be more feeble, are necessary.

And those [members] of the body which we think to be less honorable, upon these we bestow more abundant honor; and our uncomely [parts] have more abundant comeliness.

For our comely [parts] have no need: but GOD has tempered the body together, having given more abundant honor to that [part] which lacked. That there should be no schism in the body; but [that] the members should have the same care one for another.

And whether one member suffer, all the members suffer with it; or one member be honored, all the members rejoice with it.

Now you are the body of Christ, and members in particular (1 Cor. 12.12-27).

Being all of the same source, the five divisions are members of one body though given to different expressions:

For as we have many members in one body,

and all members have not the same office: So
we [being] many, are one body in Christ and
every one members of one another (Rom.
12.4-5).

Jesus referred to this when he said:

Inasmuch as you have done (it) unto one of
the least of these my brethren, you have done
(it) unto me... (Matt. 25.40).

Herodotus (102) also stated that the Egyptians before the reign of
Psammetichus thought that of all races in world they were the most
ancient. When Psammetichus came to the throne he decided to settle
the question. He gave two new-born infants to shepherds to be brought
up with the orders that no one should utter a word in their presence so
that he would see in which language they would first speak. Two years
later the first word the children spoke was becos, the Phrygian word for
bread. Based on this the Egyptians yielded their claim of being the
oldest race. In his view, Herodotus felt there was no need for the experiment with the children because he said the Egyptians existed ever since
men appeared on the earth (Herodotus 107).

According to Genesis, the primal divisions of the adamic race
appeared simultaneously in the earth, as projections of the first-born.

And the LORD GOD took the man (adam)
and put him into the garden of Eden to dress
it and keep it (Gen. 2.15).

The LORD GOD, the first-born, had already put the man whom he
had formed in the garden eastward ("in the front, to project oneself") in
Eden (Gen. 2.8), now that the consciousness of the five senses, by which
the physical being would function, had been projected, mankind (adam)
was placed into the garden, or gardens (Garden: "gan" is also translated
as a plural) to dress (serve, till) it.

On the collective level in the earth and on the individual level in the
body, the adamic race was now settled in the habitation with the ability
to function by the five senses.

And the LORD GOD commanded the man
(adam) saying, Of every tree of the garden,
you may freely eat.

> But of the tree of the knowledge of good and
> evil, you shall not eat of it: for in the day that
> you eat thereof dying you shall die [8] (Gen.
> 2.16-17).

The first adamic root race now functioned independently under the command of the attuned consciousness, the LORD GOD, but with free will. Every tree of the garden (which was pleasant to the sight and good for food, and of which the Assyrian was one) represented the expressions, or activities, of consciousness with the individual body, and with the collective body (the five divisions of the race). They were free to partake of the expressions of consciousness of the LORD GOD in the body and in the world: they were free to intermix thereby increasing the number of dominant senses in each division of the race. Each new mixture would add another dominant sense until the fifth root race is reached when all five senses would be heightened.

The tree of the knowledge of good and evil symbolized the duality represented by the sons of men and the race of Nephilim who had experienced "good and evil" in the earth. Knowledge is information retained in the memory bank, the sub-conscious mind. The intellect, like the body, was in a clean state, a tabula rasa, but actions would be retained in the memory and ingested into the system. From within, the new race was forbidden from intermixing with the pre-adamic races, and was warned that if duality is experienced and division takes place in consciousness (day), spiritual death (loss of contact with the Omnipresent Consciousness) would follow and lead to physical death.

Programming Man

The loosely-knit "dust" body was completed and self-sustaining. The adamic beings were in tune with higher consciousness and equipped with five senses on the physical level. These new inhabitants of the planet would have the sensitivity and instincts that characterize the red division of the race (feeling of the collective body), the orderliness and understanding of the yellow (hearing of the collective body), sustaining quality and sensuousness of the black (tasting of the collective body), the perception and desires of the white (seeing of the collective body), and the awareness and self-consciousness of the brown (smelling of the collective body). But, as yet, they were all the same and without emotions or experience.

---

[8] Gen. 2.17, KJV margin.

> And the LORD GOD said, It is not good that
> the man (adam) should be alone. I will make
> an help meet for him (or aid as before him)[9]
> (Gen. 2.18).

Alone here is "bad," which also means "a part of the body, a branch of a tree, and of each alike," and conveys a dual meaning. And help meet is exer: "aid," from azar: "to surround." In the creation by GOD in Genesis One everything was deemed "good." Here, an assessment is made by the inner being that being alone is "not good."

> And out of the ground the LORD GOD for-
> med every beast of the field, and every fowl of
> the air (heaven), and brought (them) unto
> Adam (mankind)[10] to see what he would call
> them; and whatsoever Adam (mankind) called
> every living creature, that was the name
> thereof (Gen. 2.19).

Beast and fowl had been brought forth on the "fifth day" before the creation of the images of mankind. Where Ezekiel wrote of the Assyrian as a tree, he continued:

> All the fowls of heaven (air) made their nests
> in his boughs, and under his branches did all
> the beasts of the field bring forth their young
> (Ezke. 31.6).

Every beast of the field and fowl of the air, which were formed out of the adamah, represented animal instincts, mental, emotional and physical attributes. The "living creatures" symbolized in the adamic race what the hybrid composite beings like the Cherubim symbolized in the earth -- the expressed thoughts. The attributes are those associated with certain beasts and fowl:

---

[9] Gen. 2.18, KJV margin. LB reads: "a helper who is like him." NEB reads: "a partner for him," and NAB reads: "a suitable partner for him."

[10] KJV & LB list the original word capitalized: Adam: "mankind, human being," and MT, NAB & NEB list "the man" which is also adam: "mankind, human being." The original is the same word that has been used so far. It does not change to a proper name until later in the text.

Beasts	Fowl
Meek as a Lamb	Wise as an Owl
Friendly as a Dog	Peaceful as a Dove
Stubborn as a Mule	Vain as a Peacock
Greedy as a Pig	Crazy as a Loon
Sly as a Fox	Happy as a Lark

Some of these attributes can be applied on two levels. We can be as wise as an owl (intellectually wise) or as wise as a serpent (worldly wise). When we have flights of fancy, then we are high minded. When we become indifferent we bury our heads in the sand like an ostrich. We can be swift as a deer, clumsy as an ox, fierce as a tiger, shy as a mouse, nervous as a cat, angry as a bull, timid as a rabbit, smart as a hawk and eager as a beaver. We can laugh like a hyena, crow like a rooster, roar like a lion, or sing like a canary, etc. As living creatures made out of the adamah, the attributes freely named are seen as a real force. Some of the most visible effects of attitudes and emotions on our chemistry are tears when we are sad, trembling when we are afraid, blushing when we are embarrassed, perspiring when we are anxious, etc. Other effects that occur within are called psychosomatic. This is expressed in Proverbs (23.7) as, "For as he thinks in his heart,[11] so is he."

The thoughts were formed by the unified inner being (the LORD GOD) and expressed (named) by the outer being.

> And Adam (mankind) gave names to all cattle, and to the fowl of the air and to every beast of the field: but for Adam (mankind) there was not found an help meet for him[12](Gen. 2.20).

Separation of the Polarities

The original light that became the image is the total force, male/female, active/receptive, positive/negative polarities (the yin/yang). While adam is a generic term, it is also used to distinguish the first human beings in the species: "Male and female created he them, and blessed them and called their name Adam: mankind, human beings" (Gen. 5.2). In the Babylonian story of creation, the first human being is

---

11 Nephesh. MT reads "within."
12 LB reads: "a helper who was equal to him."

Adamu, in the Hindu (in the Prophecies) it is Adama, and in the Persian (Zend-Avesta) it is Adam.

Desire for companionship brought separation of the two principles. The text now focused on the first-born, who was the pattern for the adamic race.

> And the LORD GOD caused a deep sleep to fall upon Adam (first being), and he slept;[13]and he took one of his ribs and closed up the flesh instead thereof.

> And the rib, which the LORD GOD had taken from man (adam), made he woman, and brought her unto the man (adam).

> And Adam (mankind) said, This [is] now bone of my bones,[14] and flesh of my flesh: and she shall be called Woman (ishshah) because she was taken out of man (ish) (Gen. 2.21-23).

Now that the LORD was the inner being attuned to the Omnipresent Consciousness, GOD, the pro-creativity had come from the soul level within (deep sleep). The first being was the total force, androgynous, or neuter. The rib: tsalah, "rib (as curved)" also means an "arch" and "side," and represents half of the yin/yang, male/female circle. The Woman (ishash) was produced by the active principle. The ish: "to be extant," the active principle, symbolizes spirit (the creative force), and the masculine gender exemplifies logic and reason. The ishshah, the receptive principle, symbolizes water (the life source), and the feminine gender exemplifies intuition and emotion.

> Therefore shall a man (ish) leave his father and his mother, and shall cleave unto his wife (ishshah): and they shall be one flesh (Gen. 2.24).

---

[13] There is no mention of Adam ever being awakened. This sleep has been compared to the "sleep," or dream time of the Australian aboriginal people, who traditionally say their first ancestors lived on a barren plain during the dream time. It is also compared by some to the dream of Bhrama which we are still experiencing.

[14] NAB reads: "This one, at last, is bone of my bones." NEB reads: "Now this, at last -- bone of my bones."

The first beings in the adamic race had no physical father or mother. They were products of the LORD GOD (the father) and the Earth (the mother), the spiritual and physical. The father and mother of the ish was the total force. (Literally in hind sight, this is the second of the Ten Commandents reinforced: "Honor thy mother and thy father...")

Now that the polarities had been separated, union, or oneness, spiritually and physically will take place from the combination of the active and passive principles, the man and the woman, the ish and the ishshah in the body and in the world.

This was reiterated by Jesus (Matt. 19.5 & Mark 10.7) and expounded upon by St. Clement[15] in his second Epistle to the Corinthians in *The Lost Books of the Bible* (144).

> For the LORD himself, being asked by a certain person, When his kingdom should come? answered, When two shall be one, and that which is without as that which is within; and the male and the female, neither male nor female.

> Now t *wo are one,* when we speak the truth to each-other, and there is (without hypocrisy) one soul in two bodies.

> *And that which is without as that which is within,* - He means this: he calls the soul that which is within, and the body that which is without. As therefore your body appears, so let your soul be seen by its good works.

> *And the male with the female neither male nor female,* - He means this: he calls our anger male, our concupiscence the female.

---

[15] Clement's Epistles were publicly read in the primitive church and are included in one of the ancient collections of the Canon Scriptures. Objections to his Epistles had been raised in the Ninth Century because in them he wrote of worlds beyond the ocean and included the story of the Phoenix who rises again from his ashes to illustrate a future resurrection [i.e. reincarnation](I Cl. XII.1-9).

> When therefore a man is come to such a pass
> that he is subject neither to the one nor the
> other of these (both of which, through the
> prevalence of custom, and an evil education,
> cloud and darken the reason,)

> But rather, having dispelled the mist arising
> from them, and being full of shame, shall be
> repentant have united both his soul and spirit
> in the obedience of reason; then, as Paul says,
> there is in us neither male nor female.[16]

Consciousness of self had not yet entered and no guilt existed on the mental/emotional level.

> And they were both naked, the man (human
> being) and his wife (ishshah) and were not
> ashamed (Gen. 2.25).

Temptation

The sons of God, who had manifested as the adamic race, enjoyed their earthly paradise for an unspecified number of years before they became influenced by the life styles of those around them and became "worldly wise." This was symbolized as temptation of the woman, who represented the emotions and the receptive life source.

> Now the serpent was more subtle than any
> beast of the field which the LORD GOD had
> made (Gen. 3.1).

Reptiles (creeping things) had been made by GOD on the "sixth day." This serpent, nachash, "a snake" from nachash "to hiss i.e. whisper, to prognosticate," which was more subtle than any beast of the field (physical instincts) made by the LORD GOD, was an attribute of sense consciousness. In The Revelation (12.9, 20.2), the serpent is identified as the Satanic force (adversary), the dragon (drakon: from "to look") the devil: diabolos, "a traducer, false accuser," and deception is the most subtle trait. Jesus described this trait when speaking to his disciples:

---

[16] See Gal. 3.27-29.

> Behold, I send you forth as sheep in the midst
> of wolves: be you therefore wise as serpents
> and harmless as doves (Matt. 10.16).

Paul also equated the serpent with an aspect of duality:

> I fear, least by any means, as the serpent
> beguiled Eve through his subtlety, so your
> minds should be corrupted from the simpli-
> city (singleness) that is in Christ (2 Cor. 11.3).

Given the masculine gender, "he," the serpent is seen as the mental rationale conflicting with the intuitive force at the Omniscient (LORD) level of consciousness. LORD vanishes from the text and the serpent questions the authority of GOD, the Omnipresent Consciousness.

> And he [the serpent] said unto the woman,
> "Yeah, has GOD said, you shall not eat of
> every tree of the garden?" (Gen. 3.1).

This conversation with the serpent is typical of conversations held with one's self when facing decisions or attempting to rationalize feelings:

> WOMAN: We may eat of the fruit of the trees
> of the garden. But of the fruit of the tree
> which is in the midst of the garden, GOD has
> said, You shall not eat of it, neither shall you
> touch it, lest you die (Gen. 3.2-3).

The command not to eat of the fruit of the tree in the midst of the garden had been to the androgynous being (Gen. 2.17) before the separation of the ish and the ishshah, therefore the woman (the ishshah), the twin soul of the man, was aware of the prohibition. The androgynous being had not been prohibited from touching it because such a command was not applicable to the neuter being: touch, naga: "lay the hand upon" is also a euphemism for "laying with." Fruit: periy, also means, "reward," and conveys a dual meaning here: the activities and the results of the activity. The fruit of the tree in the midst of the garden symbolizes results of activities of the constructive and destructive forces. In the body, it is represented as the impulses of the vagus, "wandering," nerve. (See figs. 2 & 3) This nerve has more extensive distribution than any other cranial nerve. It passes through the neck and thorax to the abdomen. At the solar plexus it further gains connections through filaments with the hypogastric and pelvic plexuses. It is composed of motor and sensory fibers, both efferent (outgoing), which are anabolic in action (they synthesize, or construct), and afferent (incoming), which are catabolic in action (they break down). Source of the afferent fibres of the vagus is in the solar plexus. Its two semi-lunar ganglia, called the abdominal brain, reach the vagal center of the medulla. All the vital forces are more or less under the control of the vagus nerve and its center. While the vagus has autonomic action, its impulses can be triggered by attitudes and emotions!

In *The Mysterious Kundalini* (45-54), Vasant G. Rele compares the vagus nerve to the yogic "Kundalini system," the centers of vital energy, the way by which one may gain control over the autonomic nervous system. While the activities of the vagus are automatic and unconscious, it is possible to bring these activities under control of the will, thereby gaining complete control over the vital forces of the body.

Activities of the constructive and destructive forces in nature had been experienced by the gods on the collective level, but not yet by adamic beings in the body:

> SERPENT: You shall not surely die: for
> GOD knows that in the day you eat thereof,
> then your eyes shall be opened, and you shall
> be as gods (Elohiym), knowing good and evil
> (Gen. 3.4-5).

Eyes: ayin, which also means "fountains or springs,"[17] conveys a double meaning here: desire, and the waters of life: the hormonal secretions. To consciously eat of the fruit of this tree is to divide the purpose in the earth and the impulses in the body. (If one could consciously gain control over the vagus nerve, one would be like a god with control over the vital functions.)

> And when the woman saw that the tree was
> good for food, and that it was pleasant to the

---

[17] Compare ayin: "fountain," Gen. 16.7, Deut. 33.28, 2 Sam. 29.1, Neh. 2.14, 3.15, Num. 33.9, 2 Chron. 32.3 & Prov. 8.28.

Way of the Tree of Life in the Body

Fig. 2 - Autonomic Nervous System showing six plexuses of the Sympathic System and course of the Vagus Nerve

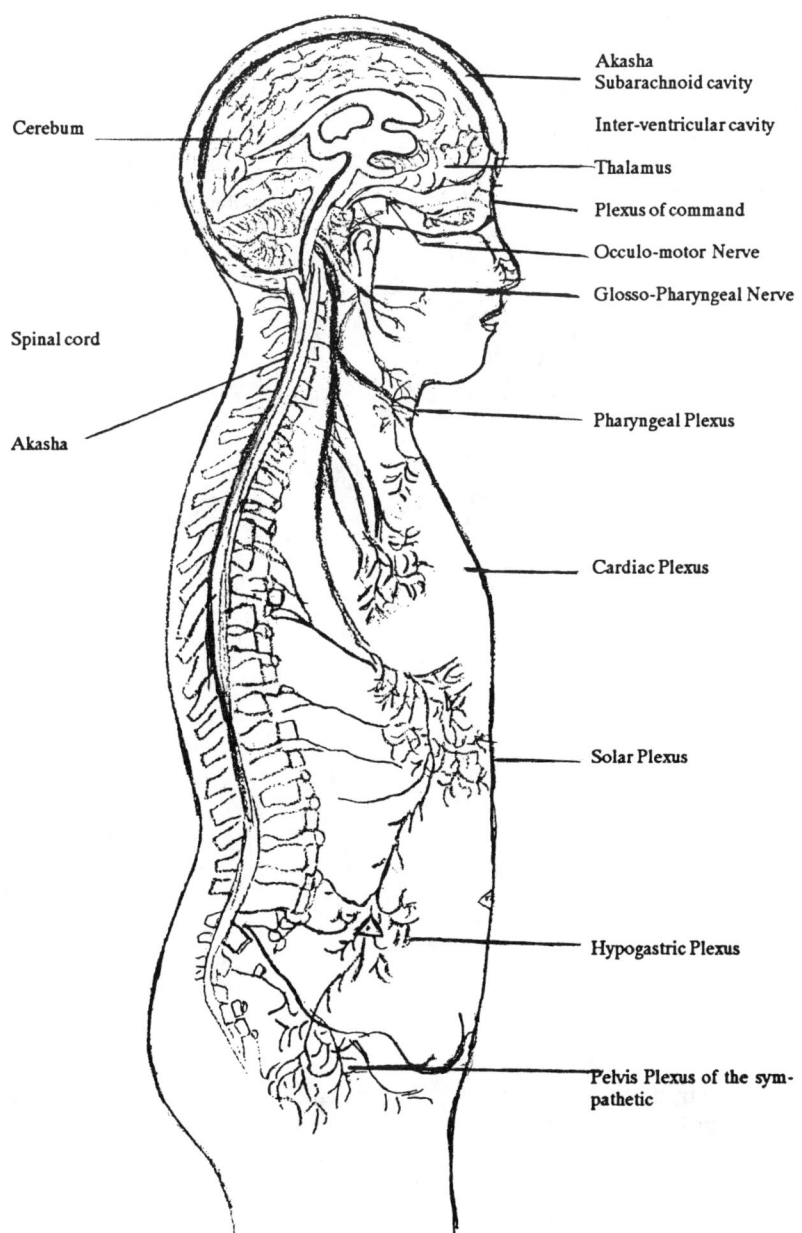

Akasha
Subarachnoid cavity

Cerebum

Inter-ventricular cavity

Thalamus

Plexus of command

Occulo-motor Nerve

Glosso-Pharyngeal Nerve

Spinal cord

Pharyngeal Plexus

Akasha

Cardiac Plexus

Solar Plexus

Hypogastric Plexus

Pelvis Plexus of the sympathetic

Way of the Tree of Knowledge of Good and Evil

Fig. 3 - The Vagus "Wandering" Nerve

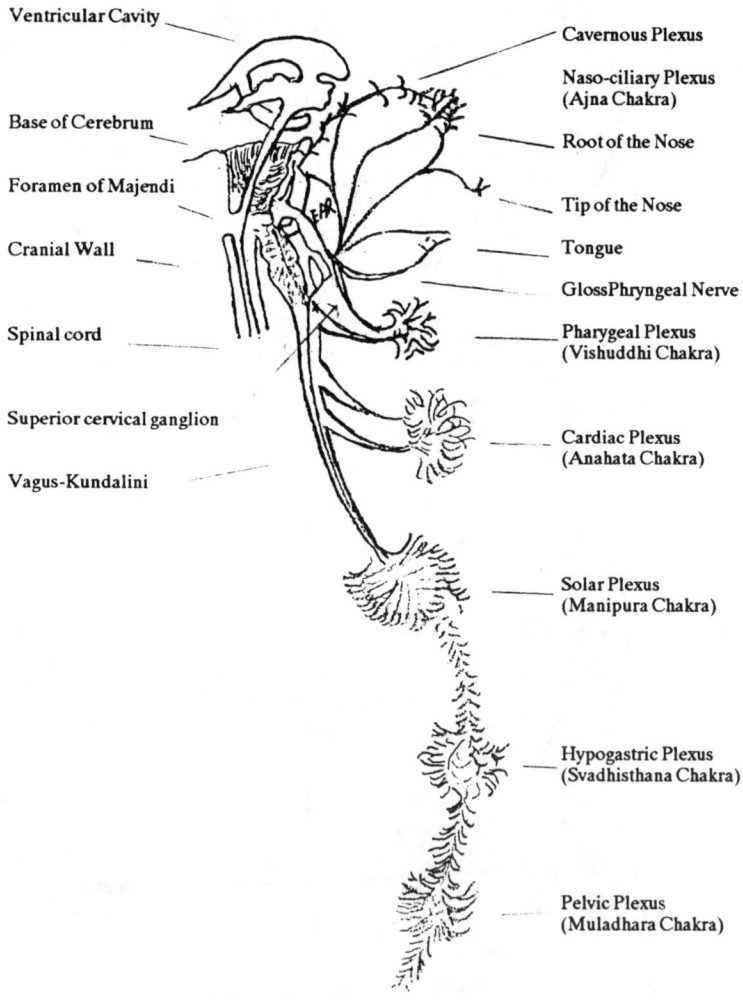

Ventricular Cavity

Base of Cerebrum

Foramen of Majendi

Cranial Wall

Spinal cord

Superior cervical ganglion

Vagus-Kundalini

Cavernous Plexus

Naso-ciliary Plexus
(Ajna Chakra)

Root of the Nose

Tip of the Nose

Tongue

GlossPhryngeal Nerve

Pharygeal Plexus
(Vishuddhi Chakra)

Cardiac Plexus
(Anahata Chakra)

Solar Plexus
(Manipura Chakra)

Hypogastric Plexus
(Svadhisthana Chakra)

Pelvic Plexus
(Muladhara Chakra)

Origin, connection and arrangement of the Afferent and Efferent Fibers of the Vagus Nerve.

> eyes, and a tree to be desired to make one
> wise, she took of the fruit thereof, and did eat,
> and gave also unto her husband (ish) with her:
> and he did eat (Gen. 3.6).

The senses transmitted desires to the mental (ish) via the emotions (ishshah).

Self Consciousness

The cliche, "Ignorance is bliss," aptly describes the state of the first root race before the influence of the physical senses and appetites were felt. Seeing, tasting, and touching, personified by the white, black and red divisions of the race, had now been experienced.

> And the eyes of them both were opened, and
> they knew that they were naked: and they
> sewed fig leaves together, and made them-
> selves aprons (Gen. 3.7).

Now that the "waters of life," the hormonal secretions, were opened on the physical level, they were aware of their sexuality. In The Revelation, the leaves of the tree are for healing. Addition of the fig leaves to the "dust body" followed the first self-willed, or voluntary, actions and symbolized the leaf-like foldings, the lamellae, of the cerebellum in the developing body. (The reactions of the cerebellum are "unconscious." All of its functions are not known, but it is associated with voluntary actions. When damaged, physical imbalance occurs. However, persons with congenital absence, either total or partial, have been found to have no nervous defects.)

When awareness on the physical level took place, self-consciousness entered. Concealment of the thoughts and emotions, and the original state of the "dust" body began. Psychologically, the covering of leaves represented a defense mechanism, a way of repressing memory. (Elimination from the regenerated body of the last Adam of unproductive voluntary actions that bring self-consciousness was symbolized by Jesus (Matt. 21.19). When he saw a fig tree in the way with leaves, but no fruit, he withered the tree.)

Separation from the source had begun and the balance of the body was in jeopardy.

> And they heard the voice (or sound) of the
> LORD GOD walking in the garden in the
> cool of the day. and Adam (generic man, not
> the individual) and his wife hid themselves
> from the presence (face) of the LORD GOD
> amongst the trees of the garden (Gen. 3.8).

The place where the transgressions of the adamic being were hidden are compared to the bosom by Job (31.33). Cool here is ruwach: "spirit, wind, breath, mind," and day is symbolic of the light, a period of awareness and the constructive force. The sound of the inner being was heard as the voice of conscience, the Spirit of Truth. The face of the LORD GOD, which had been hidden from, is the seat of the attuned consciousness, "the secret place of the Most High" in the kingdom of heaven within. The adamic being had forsaken the command of higher consciousness and had succumbed to the outer senses. The force had now fallen from the heavenly level (head) to the earthly level (the thorax), and the inner being now became aware of the separation of the ego (I, self, LORD).

> LORD GOD: Where are you?

> HE (Adam): I heard your voice in the garden,
> and I was afraid because I was naked, and I hid
> myself (Gen. 3.9-10).

Fear and self-consciousness registered in higher consciousness truthfully. He here: hiy also means "self."

> HE (LORD GOD): Who told you that you
> were naked? Have you eaten of the tree,
> whereof I commanded you that you should
> not eat?

> MAN: The woman that you gave [to be] with
> me, she gave me of the tree, and I did eat
> (Gen. 3.1-12).

The conscience is placated and the lack of will and self control justified by shifting the blame to the receptive principle (the emotions), which also has to answer to higher consciousness.

LORD GOD: What is that you have done?

WOMAN: The serpent beguiled me, and I did
eat (Gen. 3.13).

Emotions are truthfully recorded, and the reprobate mind (the serpent) is blamed and cursed by the attuned consciousness.

The Curses

LORD GOD: Because you have done this,
you are cursed above every beast of the field:
upon your belly shall you go and dust shall you
eat all the days of your life (Gen. 3.14).

The serpent, which was once in the mental realm, the heavenly level of the body, was now cursed to fall to the earthly level of the body, to the "abdominal brain," where it would be mobile (shall go) and would be sustained by the forces of creativity (dust). This will be a permanent condition as long as man is on the physical level (all the days of your life). Symbolically, Moses will raise up this "serpent" in the wilderness and Jesus will compare it to lifting up the fallen son of man (John 3.14). The early Egyptians portrayed the serpent as being lifted up in their headdresses and in the Yogic tradition the serpent represents the kundalini, the dormant power resting coiled at the base of the spine, which must be lifted up before true union is achieved. Two "lifted up" serpents are twined around the caduceus, the winged staff of Hermes.

Conflict between the woman (intuition, emotion, the life source) and the serpent (rebellion, deception, temptation) will accompany this fall.

LORD GOD: And I will put enmity between
you and the woman, and between your seed
and her seed: it shall bruise your head, and you
shall bruise his heel (Gen. 3.15).

This enmity will become part of the fall into matter, and contention between the adamic race (seed of the woman) and the Satanic forces (seed of the serpent) will become a set pattern. Conditions were now imposed on the receptive principle.

> HE (LORD GOD): I will greatly multiply your sorrow (itstsabown) and your conception; in sorrow (etseb) shall you bring forth children: and your desire shall be to your husband, and he shall rule (have power) over you (Gen. 3.16).

The two kinds of sorrow here: itstabown: "worrisomness, pain, anger, from atsab: "to carve, fabricate or fashion" and etseb: "an earthen vessel, pain of body or mind" refer to the physical and mental pain. The emotional nature (and female hormones) will be increased and creativity on the spiritual and physical levels will take place from the combined efforts of the man and the woman, the ish and the ishshah, the spirit and the water (not unilateral or asexual as had been with separation of the polarities. This condition will not be permanent (not "for all the days of her life") as was the curse that will befall the serpent force. The woman's chemistry will change in later life. Also as part of the curse, logic will rule over the intuitive nature.

Although the conditions imposed on the woman were not permanent, as long as the man and the mental rationale are predominant, the woman, the intuition, will be subdued. The original state of the adamic race will not be regained on the individual level in the body and the collective level in the earth until these two forces are again equal. Asexual reproduction will not take place again until the ish and ishshah, the spirit and the water are united in one body (as was with Mary, the mother of Jesus).

The text focuses again on the original being, indicating that Adam was the first of the sons of God to fall.[18]

> HE (LORD GOD to Adam): Because you have hearkened unto the voice of your wife, and have eaten of the tree, of which I commanded you, saying, You shall not eat of it: cursed is the ground for your sake; in sorrow shall you eat of it all the days of your life (Gen. 3.16).

---

[18] See 1 Cor. 15.22.

Because Adam did not exercise his will properly, but followed his emotional desire, he brought imbalance to the body. Mental anguish (sorrow) will be fed into the system as long as man is in the physical (all the days of his life).

> LORD GOD: Thorns and thistles shall it bring forth to you: and you shall eat of the herb of the field (Gen. 3.18).

Pain and disease (thorns and thistles) will accompany imbalance in the body and drain the sustaining forces (herbs of the field). Thorns and thistles also symbolize rebellious offspring and unproductive efforts.

> LORD GOD: In the sweat of your face shall you eat bread, till you return unto the ground: for out of it were you taken: for dust you are and unto dust shall you return (Gen. 3.19).

Bread is called "the staff of life." This bread, which will be produced in the sweet of the face (aph[19] -- where the LORD GOD breathed the breath of life) symbolized the "bread of life" (the bread of God, the bread of heaven).[20] Sweat in the face represents glandular excretions of moisture. The temple of God, the heavenly level of the kingdom within, is in the head. The two higher levels of the kingdom within are symbolized as the "most holy," the seat of the Omnipresent Consciousness (GOD -- Father or Parent) and the pituitary gland, and the "holy place," the seat of the Omniscient Consciousness (LORD -- Son or Child) and the pineal gland. When we are spiritually aware, when we raise our inner force, activity of both these glands are felt in the face (in the forehead and at the bridge of the nose). The master gland, the pituitary, controls the other glands of the endocrine system (See figs. 4 & 5). Secretion of hormones from these glands are necessary to sustain life. The full extent of the power of the master gland is not understood at this time, but it is currently being studied. The human growth hormone secreted from the pituitary stimulates bone growth and skeletal development, accelerates the production of DNA (deoxyribonucleic acid) and RNA (ribonucleic acid): the two master chemicals of heredity, stimulates the manufacture

---

[19] The front of the face; aph,"nose or nostril; hence the face." From Anaph; "to breathe."

[20] See John 6.32, 35, 48, 50, 51 & 63.

The Seven Centers of the Spiritual Body

Fig. 4 - The Endocrine System

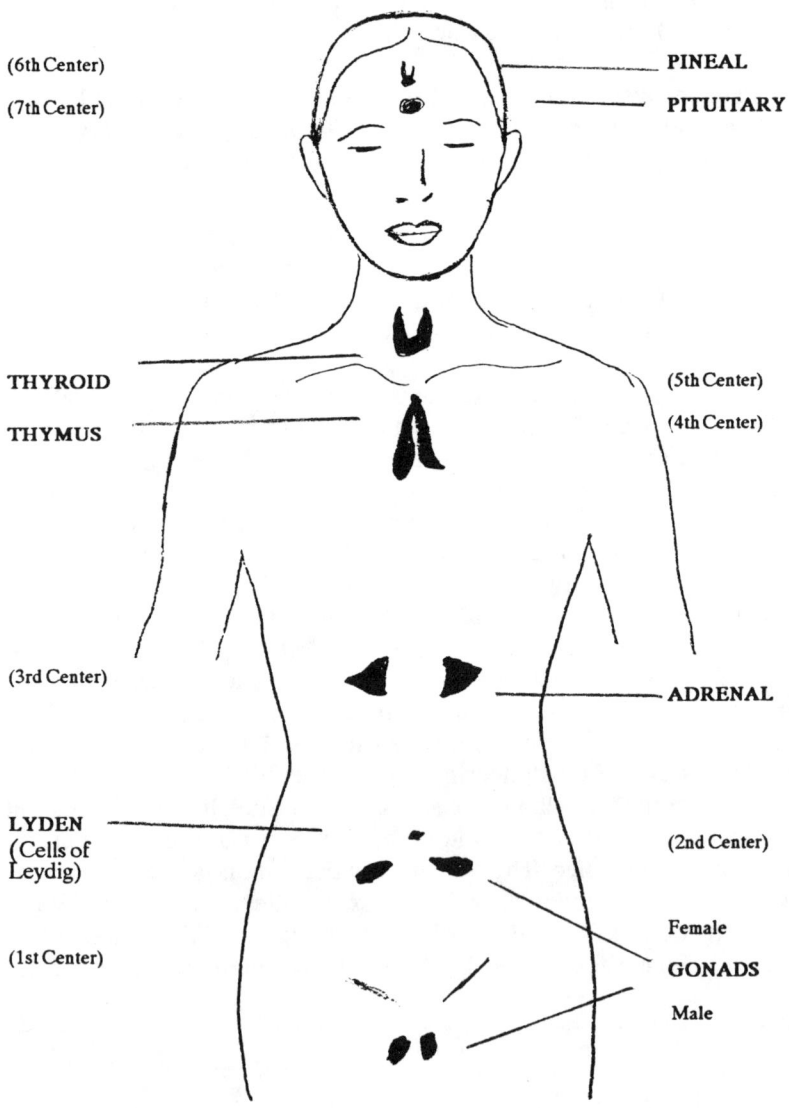

(6th Center) — PINEAL

(7th Center) — PITUITARY

THYROID — (5th Center)

THYMUS — (4th Center)

(3rd Center) — ADRENAL

LYDEN
(Cells of
Leydig) — (2nd Center)

Female

(1st Center) — GONADS

Male

The Seven Chakras

Fig. 5 - Sanskrit names and symbols for the seven spiritual centers

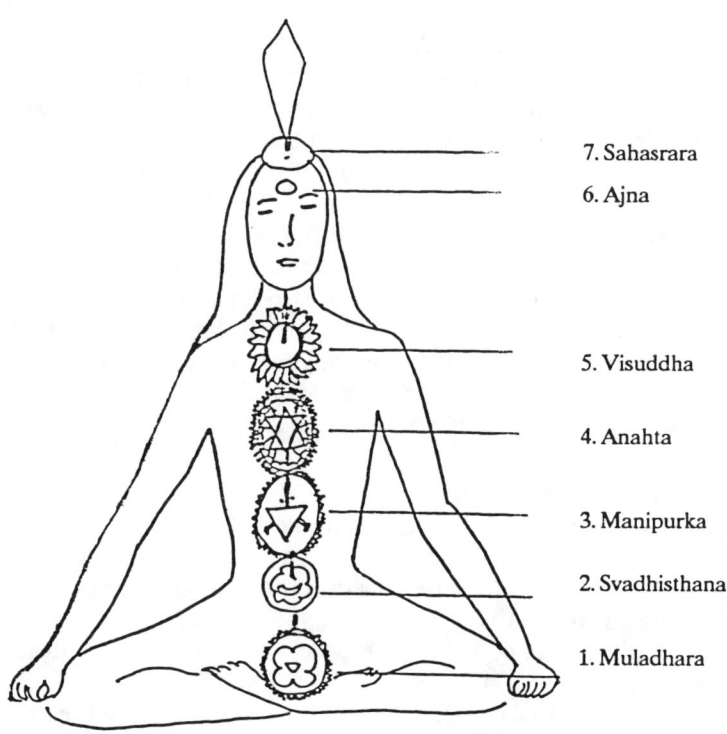

7. Sahasrara

6. Ajna

5. Visuddha

4. Anahta

3. Manipurka

2. Svadhisthana

1. Muladhara

of red blood cells and augments the flow of blood to kidneys and the rate at which the kidney does its vital filtration work, stimulates the production of protein in cells of most types, promotes formation of cells of many different types, including red blood cells, and is thought to decrease the body's stores of fat and increases muscle mass and the tissues of liver, kidney and heart.

Paul referred to the master in heaven in Ephesians 6.9 and Colossians 4.1, and Jesus gave some idea of the power of the "bread of God" when he said: "This is the bread which comes down from heaven that a man may eat thereof, and not die" (John. 6.50).[21]

The source of eternal life was now to become submerged in the body until Adam, the first-born returned to dust, the original state of the body. In the original state, as a son of God, Jesus, the first-born, said, "I am the living bread which came down from heaven: if any man eat of this bread, he shall live for ever." He compared the bread to the "flesh" of the Son of Man, and said it was spirit and life (John. 6.51, 63).

The division of the race symbolized by bread (the black) will become important in sustaining the first-born and the race, until the original state is regained individually and collectively. (In the line of Adam, Abraham [Gen. 12.10], Joseph, [Gen. 37.28] Jacob and the rest of his family [Gen. 46.5-27] and Jesus [Matt. 2.13-14], would all be sustained and survive by going into Egypt, the land of "the black.")

Death and Rebirth Enter

Man was told that in the day that he ate of the tree of the knowledge of good and evil that he would die. Yet, he did not die physically at that time. Instead, he became imprisoned in the body. Allegorically, in the Bible, "prison" refers to bondage in the physical body, and "the dead" to the fallen man. (Hence Paul's reference to baptism for the dead (the fallen self) (1 Cor. 15.29). The first death was spiritual.

With the spiritual death, the cycle of physical death and rebirth was set in motion and became the inheritance of man:

For as by one man sin entered into the world, and death by sin: and so death passed upon all men (Rom. 5.12).

While the physical man is perishable, the light of man, the inner LORD that was brought forth in the beginning, is eternal: "though our outward man perish, yet the inward man is renewed day by day" (2 Cor. 4.16).

Both the spiritual and the physical were now bound to return to dust: the physical man when the bodies expires and the spiritual man

---

[21] Also see John 6.33.

when the spirit, the inner Lord, returns in a new body:

> [Lord] you take away their breath, they die,
> and return to their dust. You send forth your
> spirit, they are created: and you renew the face
> of the earth [adamah: ground] (Ps. 104.29-30).

In his Messianic prophecy, Micah wrote:

> But thou Bethlehem Ephratah, though you be
> little among the thousands of Judah, yet out
> of you shall he come forth unto me that is to
> be Ruler in Israel: whose goings forth have
> been from of old, from everlasting (Mic. 5.2).

The cycle or rebirth in the earth of the eternal essence, the return to the womb, is described in Job: "naked came I out of my mother's womb and naked shall I return there" (Job. 1.21). However, this cycle will not be completed until the dead, the fallen man, is resurrected and the original state regained. Until then, the ishshah, the receptive principle, the life source, the water, will be the channel of spiritual and physical rebirth and was recognized as the life-giver by mankind.

> And Adam (mankind) called his wife's name
> Eve (Chavvah: "life giver"), because she was
> the mother of all living (Gen. 3.20).

As a son of God, like Melchizedek and later Jesus, adamic man was originally above the laws of nature possessing naturally all the abilities that are now termed paranormal, psychic, or extra-sensory. The fall into materiality took place in stages. The first separation came with rebellion against the command of the attuned consciousness, when Adam hid himself in the "garden" and covered himself with fig leaves. This resulted in opening of the "waters of life" on the physical level and the "curses." Another development now took place in his loosely knit "dust" body.

> Unto Adam (mankind) also and to his wife
> did the LORD GOD make coats of skins, and
> clothed them.

And the LORD GOD said, Behold, the man (the human being) is become as one of us (or exists united), to know good and evil: and now, lest he put forth his hand, and take also of the tree of life, and eat, and live forever.

Therefore the LORD GOD sent him forth from the garden of Eden, to till (serve) the ground from whence he was taken (Gen. 3.21-23).

The duality that had been experienced by the sons (or children) of men before the entrance of the ideal form had now been repeated by the adamic beings at the ego level of sense consciousness. The adamic race now also became trapped in the physical, as their predecessors had been, by a covering made by the inner man. The coats of skin symbolized the developing cerebellum which is concerned with muscle coordination. Hand here is yad. "the open hand (indicating power, means, direction)" as opposed to the closed hand. Knowledge of duality and the negative and positive forces in nature, which could be used either constructively (good) or destructively (evil), coupled with access to the spirit, was a dangerous combination. The inner being, aware of the danger inherent in misuse of the god-like abilities, dispatched man (mental) and emotional, which had experienced duality, from the Omnipresent (GOD) level of the undivided consciousness, where pure "good" exists,[22] to procreate physically and to survive by physical effort.

Loss of The First Estate

So he drove out the man (human being): and he placed at the east (front, forepart) of the garden of Eden Cherubim, and a flaming sword which turned every way, to keep the way of the tree of life (Gen. 3.24).

The adamic being, who was first sent out, was now driven out of the original estate that was now protected from misuse by Cherubim, the composite "living creatures." Ezekiel stated that the king of Tyrus had been one of those Cherubim who had been perfect in his ways until iniquity was found in him (Ezke. 28.12-15). When adamic beings appeared, a very sophisticated civilization, with flying machines whose designs incorporated replicas of the Cherubim, was already in existence.

---

[22] When addressed as "Good Master," Jesus replied,"Why do you call me good? [there is] none good but one, [that is], God" (Matt. 19.16-17).

The flaming sword that turned every way sounds very much like the description of a laser-type beam.

On the symbolic level, in the body, the Cherubim represented the attributes, the animal instincts that had been named, the desires that separated adamic beings from the source of eternal life. Ezekiel described the Cherubim as composite forms having faces of an eagle, a lion, a man, and an ox, or calf (Ezke. 1.10), the same as the four beasts of the Revelation (4.7).

The calf beast is a symbol of earth, fertility, desire for propagation of the species and the reproductive organs. The man beast is a symbol of water, mental/emotional in the physical (the imaginative force), desire for sustenance, and the pit of the belly. The lion beast is a symbol of fire, energy, desire for self-preservation and the solar plexus. And the eagle beast is a symbol of air, thoughts, the desire for self-gratification and the heart. The flaming sword that turned every way represented the creative energy that could be used in either direction by the will and the active imagination.

When the adamic beings became aware of duality, wisdom and understanding (the tree of life) the unified consciousness (LORD GOD - I AM) gave way to knowledge (the tree of the knowledge of good and evil), the divided Omniscient Consciousness (LORD -- I, ego). Now, the only way to overcome the Cherubim and reach the level of the Omnipresent Consciousness where union will be regained, would be to still the active earthly forces, to "Be still and know that I am God" (Ps. 46.10).

Now that the adamic beings had "eaten" from the tree of the knowledge of good and evil, they were under the influence of both, subject to the law of cause and effect, and under the domination of the physical senses. The race would ever be confronted with the choice between the two forces until access to the tree of life was regained by uniting the force and purpose. The way had now been lost and the adamic race entered another stage in the evolutionary process.

Symbology
3. The Garden of Eden

EDEN - Original estate of the source of consciousness that was lost.

GARDEN EASTWARD IN EDEN - Original site of consciousness, source of the purposes in the body individually and collectively in the world.

TREES THAT GREW OUT OF THE GROUND - Basic patterns of action, purposes and functions of the inner man individually and collectively.

TREE OF LIFE - The autonomic nervous system in the body, wisdom and understanding of the unified consciousness.

TREE OF THE KNOWLEDGE OF GOOD AND EVIL - Constructive and destructive forces in the body and in the world previously known by the inner man.

RIVER THAT WENT OUT OF EDEN - Original stream of consciousness of the total body, sense of feeling individually in the body and collectively in the world, predominant expression of the red division of the race.

FOUR HEADS OF THE RIVER THAT WENT OUT OF EDEN. - Four divisions of the original consciousness dispersed in the world and in the body as forms of sense expressions of four other divisions of the race.

PISON - Balance, sense of hearing, predominant expression of the yellow division of the race.

GIHON - Sustaining force, sense of taste, predominant expression of the black division of the race.

HIDDEKEL - Force of perception, sense of sight, predominant expression of the white division of the race.

EUPHRATES - Discernment, sense of smell and predominant expression of the brown division of the race.

BEAST OF THE FIELD - Animal instincts.

FOWL OF THE AIR - Mental attributes.

MAN (Ish) - Active principle, logic and reason.

WOMAN (Ishshah) - Receptive principle, intuition and emotion.

SERPENT - Deceptive mental/physical rational.

FRUIT OF THE TREE - Activities and rewards of the constructive and destructive forces.

FIG LEAVES - First change in the evolving "dust" body, the leaf-like foldings, the lamellae, of the cerebellum. Psychologically, defense mechanism for suppressing memory.

CURSE ON THE SERPENT - Fall of the mental/physical to the abdominal brain.

CURSE ON THE WOMAN - Subduing of the intuition as long as the mental rationale is predominant. (Literally - Physical reproduction and menopause.)

CURSE ON THE MAN - Submergence of the source of eternal life in the body until the return to the original state. (Literally - Mental anguish, pain and disease, and survival by the physical.)

THORNS AND THISTLES - Unproductive thoughts, actions and offspring.

BREAD - Spirit and life in the physical.

COATS OF SKINS - Second change in the evolving "dust" body and the developing cerebellum concerned with muscle coordination.

CHERUBIM - Animal instincts in the physical that separate man from the source of eternal life: desire for propagation, sustenance, self-preservation and self-gratification.

FLAMING SWORD - Creative energy used in either direction.

4. Divided Consciousness

The basic story of the Bible is contained in Genesis One. What follows throughout are variations on the theme of the continual struggle between darkness and light, good and evil, the Christ Consciousness and the Satanic force, the two spirits within man and within the world.

Cain and Abel

The recurring pattern of duality was repeated in Adam's two sons who symbolized the divided consciousness individually and collectively in the adamic race in the earth, and the negative and positive impulses of the vagus nerve in the body.

> And Adam (man) knew Eve his wife, and she
> conceived and bare Cain, and said, I have got-
> ten a man (ish) from the LORD (Gen. 4.1).

The light and the images had been brought forth by GOD, the First Cause, the Omnipresent Consciousness, and the form of the adamic being had been made by the LORD GOD, the Son, the attuned consciousness. Because attunement with the Omnipresent Consciousness had been lost, GOD is now absent from the text. The LORD, the individualized Omniscient Consciousness, which had experienced "good" and "evil," stands alone as the father of Cain.

> And she again bare his brother Abel: and Abel
> was a keeper of sheep, but Cain was a tiller of
> the ground (Gen. 4.2).

A twin birth (multiple conception, which had been pronounced upon the woman) is implied here, as the account of the next child Eve bares after Abel is prefaced by "Adam knew his wife again," but not in the case of Abel.

Abel (Hebel) "transitory,"[1] personified the spiritual consciousness, the breath of life, which is transient in the earth, and symbolized the

---

[1] Also, "breath, vapor."

constructive force, the knowledge of good: truth, harmony, the light that had been separated from the darkness.

Cain (Qayin) "fixity,"[2] personified the physical consciousness that is fixed in the earth, the five senses that pertain only to the earthly experience, and symbolized the destructive force, knowledge of evil: chaos, deception, the darkness that existed before the light. Together, they represented the two spirits within man, the two uses of the creative energy in the earth, the two-edged sword, the symbolic bread and wine, the flesh and blood of the son of man.

> And in the process of time (or at the end of days)[3] it came to pass, that Cain brought of the fruit of the ground an offering unto the LORD.

> And Abel, he also brought of the firstlings of his flock, and of the fat thereof. And the LORD had respect unto Abel (or looked with favor upon Abel)[4] and to his offering.

> But unto Cain, and to his offering, he had not respect: and Cain was very wroth, and his countenance (face) fell (Gen 4.3-5).

The fruit that Cain produced from the ground, which had been cursed to bring forth thorns and thistles, and which the adamic being (mental and emotional) had been sent to till, represented undesirable actions. Jesus made this comparison when he said:

> Beware of false prophets, which come to you in sheep's clothing, but inwardly they are ravening wolves.

> You shall know them by their fruits: Do men gather grapes of thorns, or figs of thistles?

---

[2] Also, "erect, create, procure; strike a musical note; spear or lance; teach to keep cattle; provoke to jealousy."

[3] KJV margin.

[4] As in NAB. Respect is Shaah: "to gaze."

> Even so every good tree brings forth good
> fruit: but a corrupt tree brings forth evil fruit.

> A good tree cannot bring forth evil fruit,
> neither [can] a corrupt tree bring forth good
> fruit.

> Every tree that brings not forth good fruit is
> hewn down, and cast into the fire (Matt. 7.15-
> 19).

Wroth: charah, is "to glow, blaze up of anger, zeal or jealousy." Cain's actions, which were "evil" and not in harmony with higher consciousness, brought the force down from the face. Symbolically, he was "cast in the fire." Where Adam and Eve had been questioned by the LORD GOD, the attuned consciousness, the fallen being was questioned by the LORD, the Omniscient Consciousness:

> LORD: Why are you wroth? and why is your
> countenance fallen?

> If you do well, shall you not be accepted (or
> lifted up)?[5] and if you do not well, sin lies at
> the door: and unto you [shall be] his desire,
> and you shall rule over him[6] (Gen. 4.6-7).

As long as the force is fallen from the heavenly level, the body is subject to temptation of that fallen force which becomes the agent of creativity on the earthly level: "Whosoever commits sin is the servant of sin" (John 8.34). However, through right action (doing well) the fallen force can be lifted up and rule can be gained over sin. The door is the entrance to higher consciousness where attunement takes place. Jesus spoke of this when he said: "I am the door: by me if any man enter in, he shall be saved (safe)[7] and shall go in and out, and find pasture" (John 10.9).

> And Cain talked with (or challenged)[8] Abel

---

[5] As in MT Accepted is seeth, "raise up self."

[6] MT reads: "but you may rule over him."

[7] Sozo (Gk.), "safe, to save, i.e., deliver or protect (lit. or fig.) " also, "heal, preserve, do well, be or make whole."

his brother, and it came to pass when they
were in the field, that Cain rose up against
Abel his brother, and slew him (Gen. 4.8).

The powerful, negative emotion of anger produced from dis-
appointment increased to jealousy, hate, argumentativeness, and willfulness that destroyed harmony in the body and literally "slew" meek-
ness, love and righteousness, the spiritual qualities. John wrote of this:

He that loves not [his] brother abides in
death. Whosoever hates his brother is a murderer (manslayer): and you know that no
murderer has eternal life[9] abiding in him (1
John 3.14-15).

He the commits sin if of the devil, for the
devil sinned from the beginning...

Whosoever is born of God does not commit
sin; for his seed remains in him: and he cannot sin, because he is born of God.

In this the children of God are manifest, and
the children of the devil: whosoever does not
right-eousness is not of God, neither he that
love not his brother.

For this is the message from the beginning,
that we should love one another.

Not as Cain, [who] was of that wicked one,
and slew his brother. And wherefore slew he
him? Because his own works were evil, and
his brother's righteous (1 John 3.8-12).

Cain, whose jealousy and hate led him to slay his brother, was a

---

[8] Talk is amar: "to say (used widely), answer boast self, challenge, etc."
[9] Or light, the Christ Consciousness. See 1 John 5.21.

personification of the son of darkness. There was no truth in him. Jesus said to the Pharisees who did not believe his words and sought to kill him:

> You are of your father the devil, and the lusts
> of your father you will do: he was a murderer
> from the beginning and abode not in the truth,
> because there is no truth in him. When he
> speaks a lie, he speaks of his own: for he is a
> liar and the father of it (John 8.44).

When Adam and Eve had been confronted by their consciences they had told the truth. Here Cain lied:

> LORD: Where is Abel your brother?

> CAIN: I know not: [Am] I my brother's kee-
> per? (Gen. 4.9).

All actions are recorded truthfully in higher consciousness. There- fore, lying courts schizophrenia and does great harm. Setting up of alter- nate, false, records causes mental confusion, guilt, and separation from the truth and the light. This confusion and duality is felt by the inner self:

> LORD: What have you done? the voice
> (sound) of your brother's blood cries unto me
> from the ground (Gen. 4.10).

Though the truth was covered with a lie, it was dutifully registered. The fall of the spiritual man in the earth through misuse of the creative energy was symbolized when Cain slew Abel. The voice of Abel's blood heard crying from the ground (adamah) represented the fallen spiritual energy in the body and the submergence of the spiritual consciousness.

> LORD: And now [are] you cursed from the
> earth ground (adamah, not earth: erets),
> which has opened her mouth to receive your
> brother's blood from your hand.

> When you till the ground, it shall not hence-
> forth yield unto you her strength: A fugitive
> and a vagabond shall you be in the earth
> (Gen. 4.11-12).

Guilt from misuse of the creative ability (open hand) is ingested into the system. Vitality will be drained when the creative energy is mis-used. The curse pronounced on the serpent: to "go on his belly" (be mobile in the body), was now passed on to Cain. This is described in Job:

Now there was a day when the Sons of God (those led by the spirit of God) came to present themselves before the Lord and Satan came also among them. And the Lord said unto Satan, where did you come from? Then Satan answered the Lord, and said, From going to and fro in the earth, and walking up and down in it (Job 1.6-7).

Retribution

> CAIN: My punishment [is] greater than I can
> bear (or my iniquity is greater than that it may
> be forgiven)[10]

> You have driven me out this day from the face
> of the earth (ground - adamah): and from
> your face shall I be hid: and I shall be a fugi-
> tive and a vagabond in the earth: and it shall
> come to pass, [that] every one that finds me
> shall slay (or can slay) me (Gen. 4. 13-14).

The curse on the ground and the curse on the serpent, the Satanic force that goes "to and fro in the earth," were now in effect on Cain and the fallen man in the body and in the world:

> All manner of sin and blasphemy shall be for-
> given unto men, but the blasphemy against
> the Holy Ghost, it shall not be forgiven unto
> men...neither in this world, neither in the
> world to come (Matt. 12.31-32).

Driven from higher consciousness, the force now fell from the hea-

---

[10] KJV margin.

venly level (the face) to the earthly level in the body. There are no "free" actions. Every action brings a reaction. The doer is the ultimate recipient of the acts committed. Retribution for Cain's sin is real and will come (it shall come to pass). Obadiah stated it thus: "as you have done it shall be done to you: Your rewards shall return upon your own head" (Obad. 1.15).

The balancing effect of retribution is alluded to in such passages as:

> He that leads into captivity shall go into captivity: he that kills with the sword must be killed with the sword (Rev. 13.10).

> Be you not deceived: God is not mocked: for whatsoever a man sows, that shall he reap (Gal. 6:7).

Retribution, whether positive or negative cannot always be met in one appearance in the earth. However, there will be opportunities to overcome past mistakes. Paul stated: "If in this life only we have hope in Christ, then we are of all men most miserable" (1 Cor. 15:19).

Divine justice can take centuries and manifests collectively as well as individually. An example of how retribution manifests is illustrated in a question asked Jesus by his disciples in John 9.1-20: Jesus healed a man who had been born blind and his disciples asked whether the man or his parents had sinned. (If the man had sinned, it could only have been in a pre-natal experience since he had been born blind.)

Cain's debt owed for the murder of Abel will not be met until the time of Jesus. When speaking to the scribes and Pharisees, Jesus said:

> Upon you may come all the righteous blood shed upon the earth from the blood of righteous Abel, unto the blood of Zacharias, son of Barachias, whom you slew between the temple and the altar.

> Verily, I say unto you, all these things shall come upon this generation (Matt. 23.35-36).

Speaking of the "second coming" (which also applies individually in the body), he said that generation (who have long ago departed those physical bodies) would not pass until all (tribulations) were fulfilled

(Mark 13.30), and he added, "He who endures to the end shall be saved" (Matt. 24.13).

All actions in any given experience in the earth are recorded in the inner being at the sub-conscious (LORD) level. All actions of appearances collectively are recorded at the superconscious (LORD GOD) level. Though certain actions are not remembered, they are, nevertheless, still on file and can be reached at the subconscious and superconscious levels. Since consciousness is eternal, the records are eternal. The cumulative records of all pre-natal actions are called "the book of life"[11] (Rev. 3.5, 13.8, 20.12). Fortunately, pre-natal experiences will be hidden from the conscious mind:

> There is no remembrance of former things; neither shall there be any remembrance of things that are to come with those that shall come after (Eccles. 1.11).

Memory of pre-natal actions are felt by the conscious mind only as inclinations unless one is in touch with the Omnipresent level of consciousness. While Jesus, who was "one with the Father" remembered John the Baptist's former appearance as Elijah (Matt. 11.14, 17.12-3), John the Baptist apparently did not (John 1:21). Though Jesus said of him, "Among them that are born of women there has not risen greater than John the Baptist:" he also said: "notwithstanding, he that is least in the kingdom of heaven is greater than he." He went on to say: "And from the days of John the Baptist until now the kingdom of heaven suffered violence, and the violent take it by force" (Matt. 11:11-12).

The least in the heavenly level of consciousness, the kingdom of heaven (which Jesus said was within), is the level of the will. The will was God's gift to the images on the sixth day of creation that they may freely exercise and reap the consequences thereof. To force one's will on another being is to rob that being of the God-given gift. While Jesus, who was in attunement, said of the woman taken in adultery, "He that is without sin among you, let him first cast a stone at her" (John 8.7), John the Baptist, in his religious zeal, did not apply his will properly: he attempted to force his will on Herod Antipas and Herodias, whom he harassed and accused of adultery. He figuratively and literally lost his head.

Vengeance, or retribution, is a natural result of the law of cause and effect:

---

[11] The sanskrit Akashic Records.

> I the Lord search the heart, I try the reins,
> even to give every man according to the fruit
> of his doing (Jer. 17. 10).

> Vengeance is mine; I will repay said the Lord
> (Rom. 12:19).

Seeking vengeance results in reaping what has been sown with increase:

> LORD: Therefore whosoever slays Cain,
> vengeance shall be taken on him sevenfold
> (Gen. 4.15).

In the body, to "slay" (suppress) the physical desires instead of channelling them constructively, affects all seven levels of the spiritual system within (the four earthly and three heavenly centers): the levels of the calf beast (gonads/ovaries), the man beast (navel, pit of belly, cells of leydig) lion beast (adrenals/solar plexus), eagle beast (heart, thymus), will (throat, thyroid), the holy place (pineal), and the most holy (pituitary - the master gland).

The Mark of Cain

> And the LORD set a mark upon Cain, lest any
> finding him should kill him (Gen. 4.15).

In The Revelation, the mark received in the hand (creative ability) and in the head (five senses) distinguishes the beast. The number of the beast and the number of man are the same: 666, which numerologically equals 9, the number of the man in the Earth -- the four earthly centers of the spiritual system, and the five senses. Cain, who represented the physical man and the senses, was necessary in the material world, as the impulses of the vagus nerve are necessary in the body. In The Revelation, no one buys or sells unless he has the mark of the beast. (The literal unique mark that Cain was the first to have, because of the circumstances of his birth, was a belly button.)

> And Cain went out from the presence (face)
> of the LORD, and dwelt in the land of Nod,
> on the east of Eden (Gen. 4.16).

The physical consciousness was now predominant since the spiritual consciousness had been "slain" and the physical consciousness was in the east (front) of Eden in the land of Nod: "exile, wandering," where the Cherubim and the flaming sword were. In the body, the land of Nod is the same as the vagus nerve in the front of the thorax (vagus also means "wandering"). Cain, the fallen man, now wandered among the previous inhabitants of the earth (the Nephilim and the living creatures like the Cherubim), and the fallen force in the body travelled on the vagus nerve below the neck.

> And Cain knew his wife: and she conceived, and bare Enoch: and he builded a city, and called the name of the city, after the name of his son, Enoch (Gen. 4.17).

Cain's wife is not identified, but she could have been from the offspring of either the sons of men (the Nephilim), or of the sons of God (the adamic race), since they were contemporaries at this time. (It is more likely that she was one of the daughters of men mentioned in Genesis 6.2.)

The birth of Enoch, "initiated," ushered in development on the physical level. While the abode of the primal being had been "plant-ed" by the LORD GOD, Cain built his own city. Symbolically, the materialistic forces of creativity of the adamic race (the mark of Cain) and perpetuation of material-mindedness were now set in motion.

Seed of the Serpent

Cain's line represented the steps, or levels, of creativity of the fallen man in the physical, in the earth, and in the body:

1 - Enoch, "initiated" - beginning of creativity, pelvic plexus, gonads, propagation.

2 - Irad, "fugitive" - fallen man, hypogastric plexus, pit of belly, sustenance.

3 - Mehujael, "smitten of God" - fallen energy, solar plexus, adrenals, preservation.

4 - Methusael, "man who [is] of God" - cardiac plexus, thymus, gratification.

By the fifth generation from Enoch (the sixth from Cain and the seventh from Adam), the "bad seed" reappeared as Lamech, "strong," who represented the impulses of the pharyngeal plexus, the fifth earth center, the thyroid, the seat of the will.

> And Lamech took unto him two wives; the name of the one [was] Adah, and the name of the other Zillah.

> And Adah bare Jabal: he was the father of such as dwell in tents, and [of such as have] cattle.

> And his brother's name [was] Jubal: he was the father of all such as handle the harp and organ (pipe or reed instruments).

> And Zillah, she also bare Tubal-Cain, an instructor (forger, whetter - latash) of every artificer in brass and iron: and the sister of Tubal-Cain [was] Naamah (Gen. 4.19-22).

Lamech and his offspring were the last of Cain's descendants recorded in the Bible. Symbolically, Cain's line reached the level of the will before falling again. In the body, this represented the force rising to the neck, but falling back down in the thorax. As the father of polygamy, Lamech symbolized the adulteration of the creative impulse in the earth through self will. Activation of the materialistic forces resulted from the division of his force between Adah: "ornament," and Zillah: "shade:"

> Jabal - "a stream," the father of cattlemen, represented the force of propagation (calf beast).

> Jubal - "stream, flow" the father of musicians, represented the force of imagination (man beast).

> Tubal-Cain - "tumult? diffusion? of Cain," the father of metallurgists, represented the force of self-preservation (lion beast).

Naamah - "pleasant," represented the force of self-gratification (eagle beast).

Jabal and Jubal were the children of Adah, and Tubal-Cain and Naamah were the children of Zillah.

> And Lamech said unto his wives, Adah and Zillah, Hear my voice, you wives of Lamech, hearken unto my speech: I have slain a man to my wounding, and a young man to my hurt [or, I would slay a man in my wound, and a young man in my hurt] (Gen. 4.23).[12]

The division of purpose "slays" the creativity (slain man) and saps the vitality (young man). It is stated in Proverbs:

> whoso commits adultery with a woman lacks understanding: he that does it destroys his own soul (nephesh, which also means "vitality").

> A wound and dishonor shall he get; and his reproach shall not be wiped away.

> For jealousy is the rage of a man: therefore he will not spare in the day of vengeance: (Prov. 6.32-34).

A connection is made here between adultery (naap, which figuratively means "apostasize" and jealousy. It is conceivable that Lamech's actual crime, like Cain's, had been brought on by jealousy.

> If Cain shall be avenged sevenfold, truly Lamech seventy and sevenfold (Gen. 4.24).

Vengeance is multiplied when man does not reform. The Lord God's message for the rebellious children of Israel who would not reform was:

---

12 KJV Margin.

> If you walk contrary unto me, and will not
> hearken unto me: I will bring seven times
> more plagues upon you according to your sins:
> (Lev. 26.21).

The increased vengeance which follows a criminal is also mentioned in Proverbs: "if he (a thief) be found, he shall restore sevenfold; he shall give all the substances of his house" (Prov. 6.31). On the literal level, Lamech's fear of the sevenfold vengeance promised to anyone who slew Cain, plus increased retribution for his dual crime, suggests that it was Cain (either still alive or reborn) whom Lamech had slain.

Image and Likeness of Adam

As a balance to the physical consciousness that Cain represented, the transitory spiritual consciousness of Abel returned. When Adam was a hundred and thirty,[13] his line was re-established. He begat a son in his own likeness after his image (Gen. 5:3) (which suggests that Cain and Abel were not in Adam's image and likeness).

> And Adam knew his wife again, and she bare a
> son and called his name Seth (sheth: "substi-
> tuted, put, appointed"): for GOD [she said]
> has appointed me another seed instead of
> Abel, whom Cain slew (Gen. 4.26).

When Cain had been born, Eve said she had gotten a man from the LORD. Seth, she said, had been appointed by GOD, which means he was conceived in attunement with the First Cause and predestined. The pattern originated in the beginning had repeated: The light had manifested as the image (Adam), who fathered, by his own will, sons of men (Cain and Abel), who personified the sons of darkness and the sons of light. Misuse of the creative energy resulted in destruction of the spiritual consciousness and the fallen son of man. The individualized infinite

---

[13] The life spans recorded for the antediluvians reached up to 969 (Methuselah). Considering he began as a son of God who could have avoided death altogether, this does not seem unreasonable. The ages given for the Babylonian kings are far greater: 18,900 years for King Alulim, 36,000 for King Alalmar, etc. However, it is not certain how any of these ages were calculated, and various sources disagree on the Biblical ages. The significance of the ages appear to be in their numerological values. Both Babylonian kings are numerologically 9: man in the earth. One hundred thirty is 4: a foundation in the earth.

consciousness (Abel) was reborn in the physical by appointment of GOD and was a son of man who was a son of God (Seth).

Mortal Man and Religion are Born

The dual consciousness that Cain and Abel personified became a permanent part of man's nature with the birth of Seth's son, Enos, "mortal man."

> And to Seth, to him also there was born a son; and he called his name Enos: then began men to call upon the name of the Lord (or, to call themselves by the name of the Lord)[14](Gen. 4.26).

By the time Enos was born to Seth, the original state of the adamic being had become so obscure that it was necessary to "call on the name of the Lord" (Gen. 4.26) in an attempt to stay in touch with the infinite consciousness. This was the birth of religion for the adamic race. From this time on mortal man would continue to invent religions as a means of contacting higher consciousness. While Cain's line ushered in development on the physical level, Seth's line ushered in development on the spiritual level. The succession of Seth's line represented the opposite of Cain's. Through Cain's progeny, the initiative for physical development began with Enoch at the first level of procreation. Through the line of Seth, the initiative for the spiritual development began with another Enoch (the sixth from Seth and the seventh from Adam) at the fifth level of the will:

Cain	Seth
1 Enoch: "initiated"	1 Enos: "mortal man"
2 Irad: "fugitive"	2 Cainan: "fixed"
3 Mehujael: "smitten of God"	3 Mahalaleel: "praise of God"
4 Methusael: "man who [is] of God"	4 Jared: "a descent"
5 Lamech: "strong"	5 Enoch: "initiated"

---

[14] KJV Margin

While initiation in the line of Cain had come from the first level (propagation) and had led to the divided will, initiation in the line of Seth came from the fifth level of the will and led to a new level in the spiritual development.

Symbology
4. Divided Consciousness

CAIN - Fixed physical consciousness fallen in the Earth.

ABEL - Transitory spiritual consciousness.

FRUIT OF CAIN - Undesirable actions.

OFFERING OF ABEL - Desirable actions.

MARK OF CAIN - Creative ability through the hands and the five senses.

LINE OF CAIN - Initiation of development of materiality.

SETH - Rebirth of the spiritual consciousness in the physical.

ENOS - Mortal man seeking contact with the inner man.

LINE OF SETH - Development toward initiation of spirituality.

5. The Seventh Wonder

The first comment made about one of Adam's descendants through the line of Seth other than their ages, offspring, and that they died, was made about Enoch:

> And Enoch walked with GOD, and he was
> not: for GOD took him: (Gen. 5.22).

This sudden switch back to GOD in the text indicates that Enoch played an important role in the early story of the adamic race. Yet, there is very little information about Enoch in the Bible. The next reference to Enoch is found in the book of Hebrews:

> By faith Enoch was translated that he should
> not see death; and was not found, because
> God had translated him: for before his trans-
> lation he had this testimony (or record, wit-
> ness, report) that he pleased God (Heb. 11.5)

In Search of Enoch

The statement in Hebrews is a confirmation of the one made in Genesis with the added information that Enoch had faith and a record that pleased God. To describe Enoch's disappearance, Paul used the word, "translated:" metatithemi, "to transfer, transport, change sides," and "translation:" metathesis: "transposition, transferral, disestablishment (of a law), change."

The total information on Enoch given in Genesis and Hebrews is that he was the father of Methuselah and other unnamed sons and daughters, he walked with GOD, pleased GOD, had faith, his form was changed, and he disappeared at the age of 365.

In the book of Jude is found the only other information on Enoch in the Bible. He is quoted as having said:

> Behold, the Lord comes with ten thousands of

> his saints, to execute judgment upon all, and
> to convince all that are ungodly among them
> of all their ungodly deeds which they have un-
> godly committed, and of all their hard
> speeches which ungodly sinners have spoken
> against him (Jude 14-15).

This same statement recorded in Jude appears in an ancient manu-
script, *The Book of Enoch The Prophet* (Cashel 2), which was redis-
covered in 1773 after having been obscure for 1,500 years. This book,
along with *The Book of The Secrets of Enoch*, recounts his travels and
return, dreams, visions, communion with angels, and prophecies that
had been kept alive in oral history, and gives a possible answer to how
Enoch pleased God.

While all of Seth's other descendants had life spans of eight or nine
hundred years, then died, Enoch was "taken by GOD" at the age of 365,
the number of days in a year. In *The Book of The Secrets of Enoch* (Jack
56,57), he instructs his children that when the visible and invisible creation of the Lord ends there will be no more time, all shall be as one eon.

In The Revelation, in the symbolic process of overcoming, it is prophesied that when the seventh angel sounds "there should be time no
longer" (Rev. 10.6). The simultaneous existence of past, present and
future is expressed in Ecclesiastes 3.5: "That which has been is now: and
that which is to be has already been."

What is perceived with the conscious mind at any distance in space,
whether across the room or across the galaxy, has already been and is a
shadow of the past: The point in time and distance in space being determined by the speed of light and the motion of the observer. So we can be
conscious of various points of time at once and even perceive what no
longer exists. The further away the object is in space, the further away it
is perceived in time. For example, we see the sun as it was eight minutes
ago, the nearest star, Alpha Centauri, as it was 4.4 years ago, Arcturus,
as it was 36 years ago, Beta Andromedae as it was 75 years ago, Alpha
Crusis as it was 230 years ago, etc., and we see light of some heavenly
bodies that no longer exist, because they are so distant that the light is
just reaching us. Time, which is based on conscious perception, falls into
the realm of fourth dimensional idea. The light within travels at a faster
rate of vibration than the sense consciousness. (This is how we are able
to have precognitive dreams and visions when the senses are "asleep.")
When consciousness is at the Omnipresent level, when we "walk with
God," we transcend time and space.

For Enoch, time stopped at the completion of an earth cycle and he existed in a state of perfection. In *The Book of the Secrets of Enoch* (Jack 56), it is written that because he had been chosen by the Lord above anyone else, he would be glorified before the face of the Lord for all time. He was also said to be the one designated by the Lord to write about the invisible and visible creations, redeem his household, and be the redeemer of the sins of man. The implication of this statement is that Enoch was a return of the firstborn who would be the redeemer. He is also seen as a writer of the history of man from the beginning.

Lord of Books

Elements found in Egyptian "mythology" (such as the Phoenixes) are found in the books of Enoch and lend some credibility to the belief that when Enoch dematerialized, he re-materialized (as Melchizedek later would) in Egypt in another form.

Egypt, probably more than any other land, has had the greatest impact on Earth beings. The first five books of the Bible are attributed to Moses, a fourth generation Egyptian.

Originally part of the habitat of the black division of the race, who personify the sense of taste, Egypt became a true cosmopolitan land: all five divisions of the race are represented in their wall paintings. As the belly of the world, Egypt is the universal place of sustenance, and "going into Egypt" is a ritual in the Bible associated with physical salvation: Abraham went there to escape a famine, and the mother of his first child was an Egyptian. Joseph survived by being sold into Egypt and his wife was the daughter of an Egyptian priest. Jacob and his sons went there to escape a famine and stayed four hundred years, and Jesus was carried there as a babe to escape Herod who sought to kill him. The ancient legend that Hermes was really Idris, the Arabic name for Enoch (Bruckhardt 18), makes the theory that Enoch re-materialized in Egypt plausible, since Hermes is synonymous with the Egyptian Thoth, "god" of all arts and sciences, inventor and Lord of Books.

Thoth was called the "self-created, to whom none had given birth, god one." He was regarded as the heart and tongue of Ra and was believed to have been the author of *The Book of the Dead*, in which he is describes himself:

I am Thoth, the excellent scribe, whose hands
are pure; ...the scribe of right and truth, who
abominates wrongdoing...I am Thoth, the lord
of right and truth, who judges right and truth

for the gods; the judge of words in their essence, whose words triumph over violence. I have scattered the darkness; I have driven away the whirlwind and the storm; and I have given the pleasant breeze of the north wind unto Osiris... (Mercatante 189-190).

Hermes was credited with inventing astronomy and astrology, the sciences of number and mathematics, geometry and land surveying, medicine and botany, and with being the first to organize religion and government.

Redeeming the Sons of Men

Formation of the adamic race in the earth was to provide ideal physical forms in which the beings, who had manifested in their own thought forms, would evolve. Many of these composite forms are depicted in the art of ancient Egypt.

In *The Book of Enoch the Prophet* (Laurence 20-22), he was told in a vision to tell the Watchers (spiritual beings) that from the beginning they were made spiritual, possessing a life which is eternal and not subject to death in all the generations of the world, but that the Nephilim had been created from above of spirit and flesh by the Watchers. He was also told that the flesh of the Nephilim was to be without judgment and that he was sent to pray for them. One of the beings who accompanied him was Raphael, "healer god" (or God's healer) who presides over every suffering and affliction of the sons of men. The descendants of the Nephilim were called Raphah, "to mend by stitching, to cure, to heal, to make whole." This suggests that a change, possibly loss of the animal appendages, took place in the Nephilim through the healing arts. (Some statues and paintings show only slight hints of animal appendages, such as lambs ears.)

Much of the symbology in the books of Enoch is found in the Bible, especially in Daniel and in The Revelation, in the Dead Sea Scriptures, and in the ancient stories of the Greeks and the Egyptians. One symbol that connects these different sources is the number twelve, which appears as the twelve gates, the twelve gods, the Mazzorth, the twelve Tribes of Israel and the twelve Apostles of Jesus. Herodotus gives what he says is an eye-witness account of a place in Egypt called the "labyrinth," which he said surpassed the pyramids. It had twelve covered courts, two stories and three thousand rooms, half of which were underground. The walls were covered with carved figures, and each court was exquisitely built of white marble surrounded by a colonnade. A pyramid

240 feet high with great carved figures of animals was near the corner where the labyrinth ended, and there was an underground passage by which it could be entered (Herodotus 161).

The labyrinth that Herodotus described could well have been the prototype of a place of healing, an ancient "hospital."

It is obvious from the quote in Jude that much more was known about Enoch than is recorded in the Bible. Why so little information appears in the Bible on the first man to be "translated" could be for several reasons. The obvious one is the inherent danger of idolatry.

In his *Histories*, Herodotus (159) also stated that Egypt was ruled by "gods" before it was ruled by men, gods who lived on earth amongst men, sometimes one of them, sometimes another being supreme above the rest. The last being Orus (Horus), the Greek Apollo, the son of Isis and Osiris, the Greek Dionysus. He also said Osiris/Dionysus was 15,000 years before the reign of Amasis (570-526 B.C.).

Many of the forms of the sons of men became worshipped as "gods" and religions sprang up around them that later degenerated into animal worship. Moses and the children of Israel had been exposed to these "gods" while in Egypt. The greatest challenge faced by Moses in the wilderness was turning the children of Israel away from idolatry to the "living God" within. Inclusion of the story of Enoch as Thoth who had been worshipped as a god, and his involvement with the Nephilim could have become distorted and lead to idolatry.

It would be centuries before the Nephilim and their descendants, the Rephaim, would finally disappear. Meanwhile, the Sphinx, the sentinel of the Great Pyramid remains a silent testimony to that era.

Besides being credited with the invention of the arts and sciences, Hermes/Thoth/Enoch is credited with having been architect of the Great Pyramid (Tompkins 218).

The Great Pyramid

One of the most awesome structures built by man is the Great Pyramid of Gizeh. It was one of the seven wonders of the ancient world and continues to fascinate mankind. It has been measured from every possible angle, yet its true significance remains a mystery. There are, however, many theories. The most prevalent one: that it was a tomb, is based on an account by Herodotus (151) of a great pyramid surrounded by canals that made it an island that was built by a Pharaoh named Cheops, whose body is supposed to be buried there. However, no mummy was ever found in the Great Pyramid -- only an empty sarcophagus without a lid. In recent years, both this Pharaoh and the tomb theory have been challenged.

One of Enoch's visions in *The Book of Enoch The Prophet* could have been the inspiration for the architecture of the Great Pyramid. In the vision he proceeded to a spot where he:

> saw on the west a great and lofty mountain, a strong rock, and four delightful places.

> Internally it was deep, capacious, and very smooth; as smooth as if it had been rolled over: it was both deep and dark to behold (Laurence 28).

He was told it was a place of judgment for the sons of men until their appointed period, until Cain's seed was destroyed from the human race. He was also told that there were three separate places of judgment. (The Great Pyramid has three chambers: the Subterranean Chamber, the Queen's Chamber and the King's Chamber.)

Other theories on the purpose of the Great Pyramid are that it is an astronomical observatory, a calendar, a record of man's history written in the size, shape and colors of its stones, a place of initiation, and a useless heap of stones. Even without understanding why or how it was built, the mere fact that it is there is significant as a reminder that in "antiquity" the adamic race was highly developed. That in the second generation on Earth they had the ability to build a city as Cain had done, that the "mighty men of old" mentioned in Genesis 6.4 really existed.

In the account of construction of the Pyramid given to Herodotus, blocks of stone were taken from the quarries in the Arabian hills to the Nile where they were ferried across. It took 10 years, with 100,000 men working in three-monthly shifts to build the track along which the blocks were hauled. Building of the Pyramid itself took 20 years and the outer facing, the layer of polished limestone, was begun at the top and continued downwards (Herodotus 151). However, 30 years seems a conservative figure since a block, which averages 2.5 tons, would have had to be positioned every 91.5 seconds (Fix 42). If indeed Enoch/Hermes/Thoth who "walked with God" and had the ability to dematerialize had been the architect of the Great Pyramid, Philon of Byzantium's description of how the Colossus of Rhodes was raised could possibly have been the same method used to raise those huge blocks. He said it was raised by some miraculous force "like that used in the building of the temples of the gods" so that it was as though the figure lifted of its own accord (Walker 13). In *The Book of the Secrets of Enoch*, he is accredited with

having written 366 books. (One more than his years before translation.)
He said to his children:

> Take these books of your father's handwriting
> and read them.

> The books are many but in them you will
> learn all the works of the Lord, all that has
> been from the beginning of the Lord's crea-
> tion and what will be until the end of time
> (Jack 44).

> Thou hast seen how I wrote all works of every
> man even before his creation and all that is or
> was done by all men in all times (Jack 49).

> When comes the time of not understanding,
> then let these books I have given unto you be
> an inheritance of peace.

> Deliver them to all who want them, instruct-
> ing them that through the words therein they
> may look upon the face of the Lord (Jack 50).

According to Josephus the descendants of Seth left two records in
brick and stone. He wrote that the children of Seth were:

> inventors of that peculiar sort of wisdom
> which is concerned with the heavenly bodies,
> and their order. And that their inventions
> might not be lost before they were sufficiently
> known, upon Adam's prediction that the
> world was to be destroyed at one time by the
> force of fire, and at another time by the vio-
> lence of quantity of water, they made two pil-
> lars, the one of brick, the other of stone: they
> inscribed their discoveries on them both, that
> in case the pillar of brick should be destroyed
> by the flood, the pillar of stone might remain,

and exhibit those discoveries to mankind, and
also inform them that there was another pillar
of brick erected by them. Now this remains in
the land of Siriad[1] to this day (Josephus 27).

In *The Natural History,* Pliny (53) says that Siris was a former name
for the Nile. It is possible that Enoch's records of the history of man are
in or near the Great Pyramid and will yet be discovered as the Dead Sea
Scrolls were discovered. Herodotus (151) wrote that there are underground sepulchral chambers in the same hill where the Pyramid stands.
And in 1954 a cedar boat 140 ft. long and almost 16 ft. wide was discovered in a sealed pit at the perimeter of the Great Pyramid. More
recently, existence of a chamber under the Sphinx has been detected
sonically.

While the first Enoch, the son of Cain, initiated the building of a
city, which symbolized the beginning of building on the physical level by
the adamic race, the building initiated by the second, Enoch, who was
from the line of Seth, would have been associated with spiritual development. The books of Enoch deal with the mysteries and describe subterranean places of judgment. It is possible that the Great Pyramid was a
place of initiation into the mysteries and also a record of the past in
stone, because emblematically the descent and ascent of mankind, the
journey from light to darkness and back again to light, is portrayed in its
structure.

The Book of Life In Stone

An immediate glimpse of the records written in stone is seen before
entering the Great Pyramid. The answer to "Who am I?" is clearly laid
out in Gizeh. The Sphinx symbolizes the animal nature and the entanglement with the animal kingdon in antiquity (the same symbol as
the Cherubim), and the three pyramids symbolize the trinity. Where we
came from, what we did in the past, what we will do in the future, and
where we will go, is symbolized in the Great Pyramid. (See figs. 6, 7 & 8)

The base of the Great Pyramid represents the four corners of the
earth, and the Pyramid points to the heavens, indicating the place of our
origin. The descent into this plane as spirit is indicated by the vents that
descend from the outside of the Pyramid to the level of the King's
Chamber about 3 ft. above the floor on the north and south walls. (See
fig. 9)

The King's Chamber is approximately 19 ft. 1 in. high. Above it are
five separate compartments, called the "relieving chambers," and a
pointed roof. The roof is not aligned with the Apex of the Pyramid,

The Great Pyramid and the Sphinx

Photo by Sharda Devi

Fig. 6 - Great Pyramid and Sphinx, 1983

Photo by Sharda Devi

Fig 7 - Closeup of the Sphinx, 1983

Fig. 8 - Interior of the Great Pyramid

1- King's Chamber
2 - Empty Sarcophagus
3 - Air Vents
4 - Ante Chamber
5 - Great Step
6 - Grand Gallery
7 - Torn out floor

8 - Well Shaft
9 - Queen's Chamber
10 - Grotto
11 - Pit
12 - Blocked Passage
13 - Door

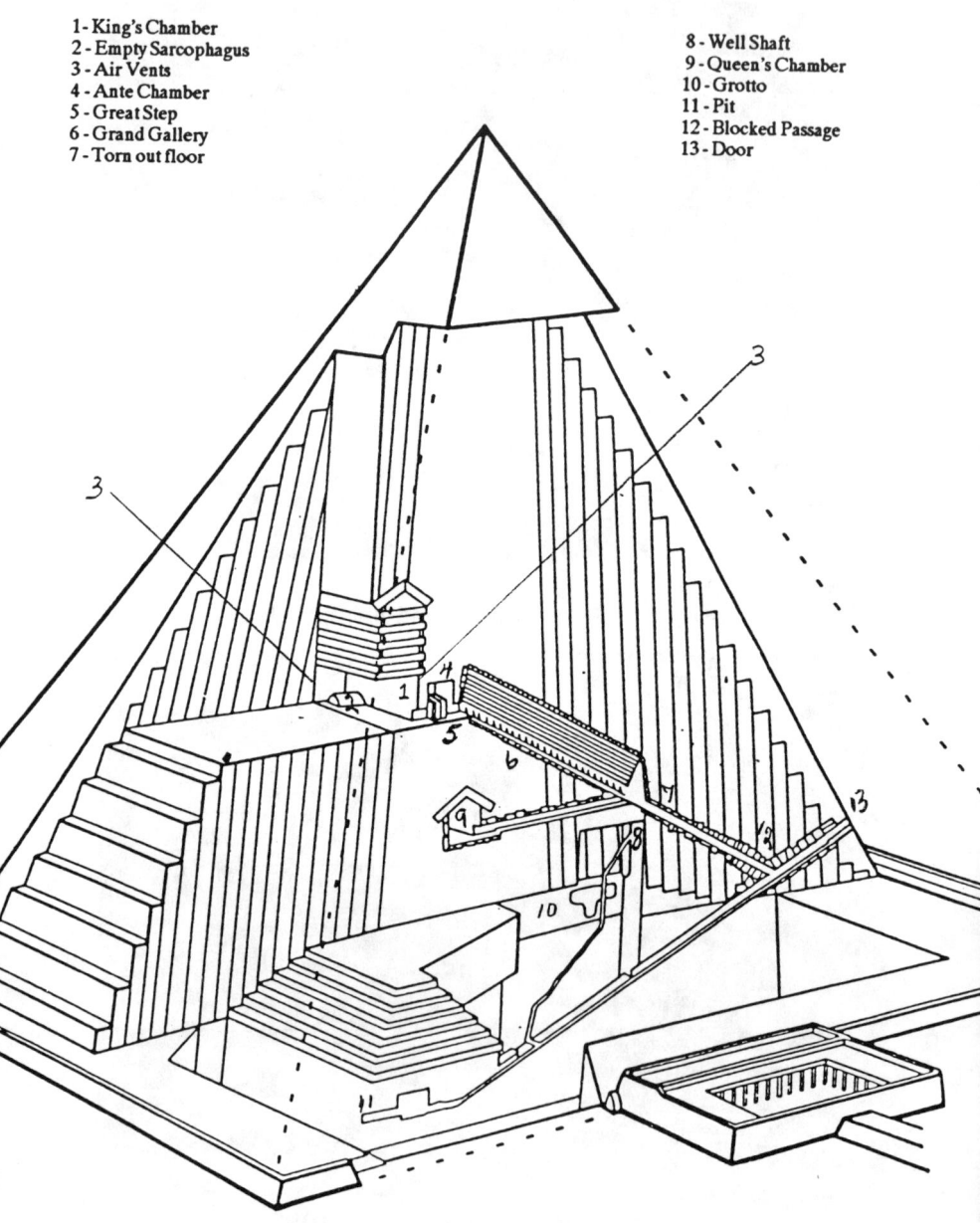

Fig. 9 - King's Chamber with Empty Sarcophagus

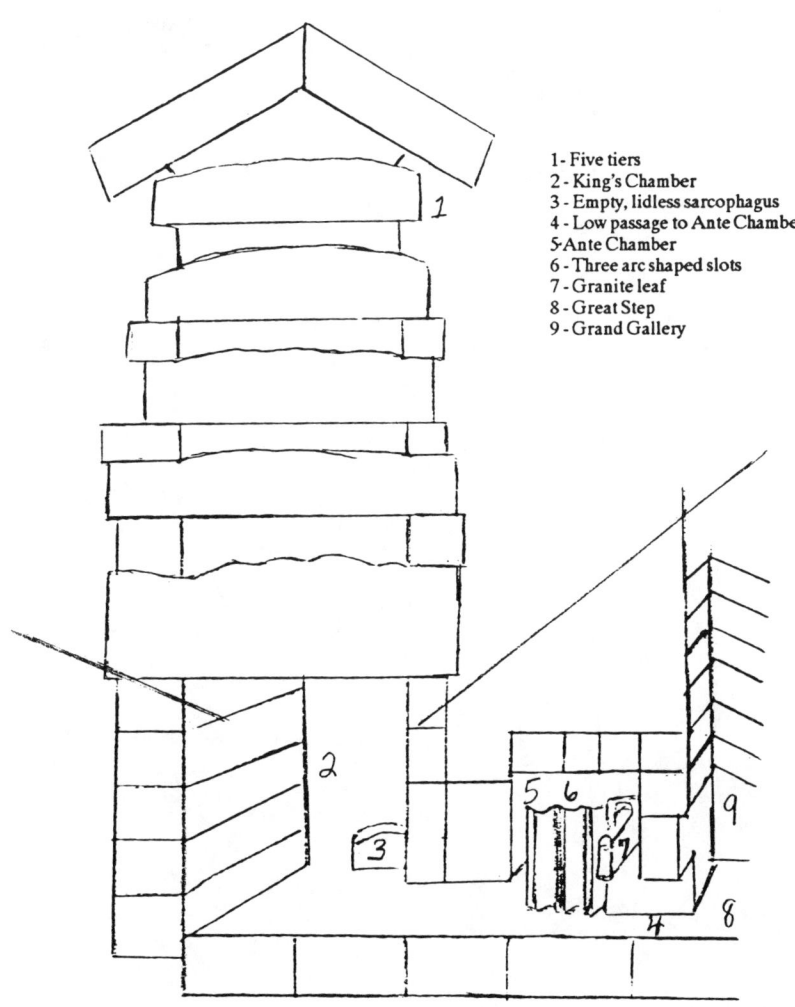

1- Five tiers
2 - King's Chamber
3 - Empty, lidless sarcophagus
4 - Low passage to Ante Chamber
5-Ante Chamber
6 - Three arc shaped slots
7 - Granite leaf
8 - Great Step
9 - Grand Gallery

Fig. 10 Queen's Chamber

1 - Five-tiered niche
2 - Alignment with Apex of Pyramid
3 - Low passage
4 - Air vents

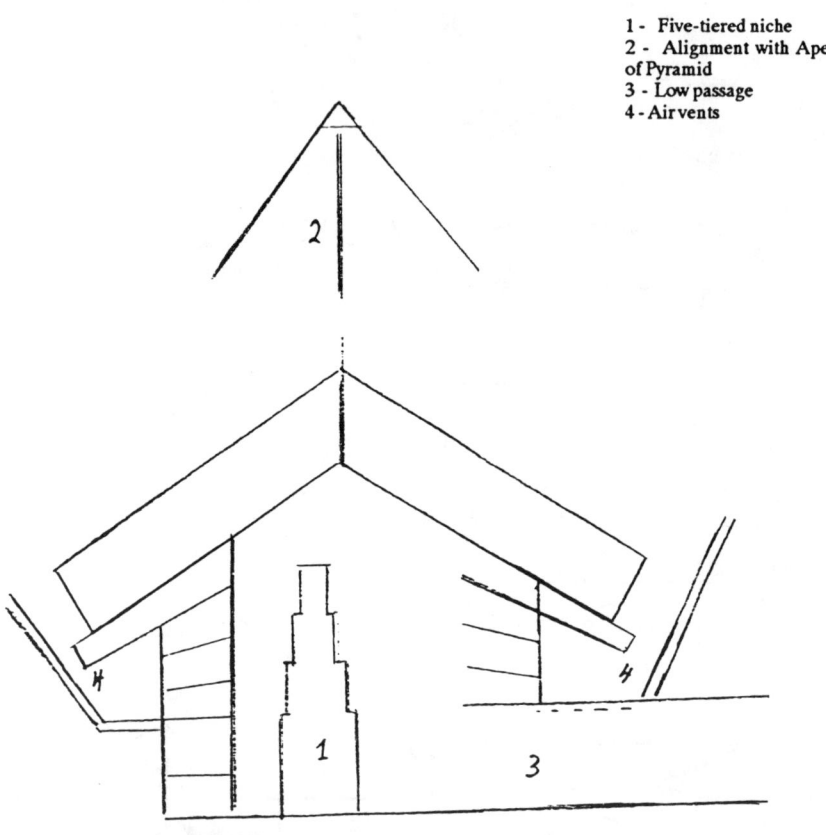

indicating that the entrance in this plane was not a specific plan.

The walls of the King's Chamber consist of five tiers of polished rose-pink granite, and near the west wall is an empty sarcophagus without a lid. The empty sarcophagus is the same symbol as Jesus' empty tomb: it signifies that there is no death at this level of consciousness. In the body, the King's chamber represents the level of the pituitary. At this stage the sons/children were still in touch with the Omnipresent Consciousness.

The next step in the descent into matter is symbolized by the Ante Chamber. Into the north wall of the King's Chamber is a low entrance to the Ante Chamber above which are three tiers of granite. Here the choice was made by the sons/children who returned to the air (the vent on the south wall) and the sons/children who entered tree dimensional consciousness (the vent on the north wall).

The low passage to the Ante Chamber is about 3 ft. high and the Ante Chamber is 12 ft. high, but only 20 inches wide. (Only one person at a time can enter.) The walls of the Ante Chamber are limestone and red granite. Three arc-shaped slots cut in both the east and west walls indicate the three dimensions and the two halfs of the yin/yang circle, the sun/moon, east/west, male/female principles. A granite leaf resembling a "gate" inserted into the fourth slot extends to the same level as the passage. The low passage terminates in a platform.

The platform is called the "Great Step." It is at the top of the Grand Gallery, which is 28 ft. high. Three feet down from the Great Step, the passage of the Grand Gallery begins. Here the great step was taken down into the earth plane and a grand period began.

The Grand Gallery grades downward and has ramps on either side into which are cut 28 holes resembling miniature sarcophagi. The two ramps represent the two spirits and the miniature empty sarcophagi indicate that death did not yet exist in these ages. The walls on each side are seven levels of overlapping stone, which represents seven levels of expression (the seven virtues and the seven deadly sins) descending into the earth.

After about 153 ft. the Grand Gallery comes to an abrupt end and drops to about 3 ft. 11 in. This passage continues to grade downward and could lead to the air, except that it is plugged up with granite blocks, which makes it a dead end. The point where the Grand Gallery ends is a juncture. Part of the floor is torn away: the descending ramp is missing a stone (on the left descending and on the right ascending) and there is a steep shaft called "the well" shaft that descends to the subterranean level. At the juncture to the left beneath the floor is another low passage that leads to the Queen's Chamber.

The violent and abrupt fall of the sons of men led by the opposing spirit is indicated by the torn out floor and the well shaft where the stone is missing that plunges downward.

Impending demise of the survivors of that civilization is indicated by the low passage that terminates in a dead end. The ramp on the side of the passage to the Queen's Chamber, represents the sons who did not fall, but found another way to evolve in the earth.

The other way, the coming of the sons of God, the creation of the ideal form of Adamic man is indicated by the Queen's Chamber (See fig. 10), which represents the level of the Omniscient Consciousness (LORD), and the pineal.

The Queen's Chamber is 18 ft. 10 in. from east to west and 17 ft. 2 in. from north to south. The interior is soft, salt encrusted limestone, and the floor, unlike the floor in the King's Camber, is rough masonry. At the opening, the walls, including the tier of the pointed roof, are seven tiers on the south and five on the north where the passage to the juncture begins. In the east wall is cut a five-tiered niche with corbelled sides that has the appearance of a tree.

The pointed roof of the Queen's Chamber is aligned with the Apex of the Pyramid indicating that this entrance was planned. The niche in the east wall indicates the "dust" body of the adamic being. (Limestone is a sandy, shaly sedimentary rock.) The seven tiers of the wall indicate the seven levels of the inner man, and the five tiers indicate the five senses.

Coming under control of the five senses is indicated at the point in the north wall where the passage becomes low. The passage leads to a short step up that lowers the passage and leads to the juncture. This is the point of the knowledge of good and evil already experienced by the gods manifested as sons of men.

The well shaft cut through the finished work indicates that it was not a part of the original plan. While the other passages are "straight and narrow," the well shaft, which extends to the subterranean level, is "crooked," indicating the serpent and the vagus nerve. At this point, the adamic being had the choice of either rising, or falling down the well shaft as the sons of men had done.

The shaft descends to the "grotto" which is above the ground level, but is of different rocks. It is a dugout and also does not appear to be a part of the original plan. Unlike the Queen and King's Chambers, the Grotto is unfinished and its roof does not point up, instead it has a depression in the floor.

Loss of the first estate of the adamic race is indicated by the Grotto, which is the place of birth of man in the physical that was "gotten from the LORD." The Well Shaft continues downward to the level of the earth and connects with a passage that descends to the Subterranean Chamber, the "pit" and another "dead end," and ascends to the juncture of the passage to the Grand Gallery, which is blocked with stones, and continues to the door that leads to the air. (This door was closed originally, but was later opened from within. In 820 A. D. a forced entrance was made about 20 ft. below the door by Al Mamoun, a Muslim Caliph. This false door is now used as the entry. The Great Pyramid is still recording and the condition of man is reflected in its condition. In the world, the forced entry represents forcible entry into the kingdom -- "climbing up the wrong way.")

At this point, the adamic race was trapped in the physical. The only way out was by somehow opening the door and entering the air about 55 ft. above the ground, or by "lifting up the serpent" by climbing up the shaft, entering the Grand Gallery, and exiting through the air vents in the King's Chamber, as spirit. This was the stage of mortal man and physical death (Adam did not die physically until long after Enos, "mortal man," was born). The pipeline of communication to the Omniscient and Omnipresent levels of Consciousness was the well shaft, through which mortals called on the name of the Lord.

Enoch was the first to rise to the Omnipresent level of consciousness and re-enter the air without "dying." However, the mortals in general were still trapped and bound with chains of darkness and still descending into matter toward the Subterranean "pit."

In the Bible, several words are translated as "pit." One is shoel: "hades, or world of the dead, as if subterranean retreat," which is also the word for "hell." In Ezekiel, where he wrote of the Assyrian being the tree in Eden, he also refers to previous catastrophes that befell the sons of men and the catastrophe that befell those in Eden who were delivered to the nether parts of the earth in the midst of the children of men.

To the end that none of all the trees by the waters exalted themselves for their height, neither shoot up their top among the thick boughs, neither their trees stand up in their height, all that drink water: for they are all delivered unto death, to the nether parts of the earth in the midst of the children (sons) of men, with them that go down to the pit.

> I made the nations to shake at the sound of his
> fall, when I cast him down to hell with them
> that descended into the pit: and all the trees of
> Eden, the choice and best of Lebanon, all that
> drink water, shall be comforted in the nether
> parts of the earth (Ezek. 31.14, 16).

He also said that those who cause terror in the land of the living will go down to the pit (Ezek. 32.18, 23-30).

Many passages in the Bible speak of "going down to the pit." And in the Bible, the "dead" and the "prisoners" bound with chains of darkness, refers to fallen mortals who are bound in the earth cycle until they return to light. Literally and figuratively, "going down to the pit," refers to being swallowed up by the earth while still alive as happened to the rebellious Korah and his men (Num. 16.30-33).

In the south wall of the Subterranean Chamber, there is an opening to a passage that terminates in a dead end. The pit indicates the fall of the antediluvian civilization and the dead end indicates the end of the descent into the physical.

In the books of Enoch, he prophesied a great destruction that was to come upon the earth and he was concerned with the preservation of his records. The Great Pyramid is located at the center of the land mass of the Earth, the navel of the world, the collective center of the Earth. As a place that Herodotus said was unaffected by changes of position of the sun, Egypt was the safest place in the world for Enoch to leave his records of the story of man. Before Enoch changed form, he fathered sons and daughters. His son Methuselah lived to be 969 years old. Methuselah's son Lamech was the father of Noah. In Noah's generation, Enoch's prophecy of a destruction would be fulfilled because by then evil had become the dominating force in the earth:

> And it came to pass, when men began to mul-
> tiply (rabab: "increase by the myriad, tens of
> thousands") on the face of the earth (ground -
> adamah), and daughters were born unto them,

> That the sons of God saw the daughters of
> men that they were fair; and they took them
> wives of all which they chose.

> And the LORD said, My Spirit shall not

always strive with man, for that he also [is]
flesh: yet his days shall be an hundred and
twenty years.

There were giants (Nephilim) in the earth in
those days: and also after that, when the sons
of God came in unto the daughters of men,
and they bare [children] to them: the same
[became] mighty men, which [were] of old,
men of renown.

And the LORD (Jehovah)[1] saw that the wickedness of man [was] great in the earth, and
[that] every imagination of the thoughts of his
heart [was] only evil continually.

And it repented the LORD that he had made
man on the earth, and it grieved him at his
heart.

And the LORD said, I will destroy (erase)
man whom I have created from the face of the
earth (ground):[2] from man unto beast and
creeping thing, and the fowls of the air; for it
repents me that I have made them (Gen. 6.1-
6).

This regret is felt and expressed by the inner man, the firstborn, the
LORD, who desired to erase the creations of the created.

The spiritual body, the image, had been created by GOD, the First
Cause, and the physical body had been made by the LORD GOD, the
attuned consciousness. After that, the beings created out of attunement
with the First Cause (with the exception of the appointment of Seth)
had been made by the LORD, the individual Omniscient Consciousness, the inner "self. The first experiment with an ideal form in which

---

[1] The word here is Jehovah, LORD. KJV translates it as GOD. ("God is not a
man, that he should lie; neither the son of man, that he should repent" (Num. 23.19).
GOD as spirit does have a physical heart.

[2] KJV margin.

God's images would evolve in the physical had gone awry because of the physical influence. The incoming sons of God had also fallen and were perpetuating the Nephilim in the earth and misusing the imaginative force. The imbalance in the physical was felt by the inner being (Heart: leb, is used widely for the feelings, will and intellect.), and guilt and remorse were felt at the Omniscient level of consciousness (LORD) because of the animal nature (the beast, creeping things and fowls made out of the ground by the Lord God) that had been expressed. Blotting out and re-programming became necessary for the next stage in the evolution of humankind on this planet.

Symbology
5. The Seventh Wonder

ENOCH - Initiation into the spiritual development.

THE GREAT PYRAMID - A record in stone of man in the earth.

THE SPHINX - A reminder of man's entanglement with the animal kingdom.

SONS OF GOD - Creations of the creator.

DAUGHTERS OF MEN - Manifestations of the created.

NEPHILIM - Thought form creations of the created.

6. End Of The Beginning

While Enoch had been at the level of the gods who were not bound by the body, Noah was at the level of the sons of men, who as sons of God, had manifested the loosely knit "dust" bodies of adamic being: he "found grace in the eyes of the Lord," and "walked with God."

An account of Noah's birth related in *The Book of Enoch the Prophet* (Laurence 175) also appears in *The Dead Sea Scriptures* (Gaster 358). Both accounts state that Noah was an unusual looking baby whose nature was not like the nature of man. He was described as looking more like the form of the son of man described in The Revelation (1.13-14). His hair was white like wool, and his eyes were like the rays of the sun. When he opened his eyes they illuminated the whole house. Because he did not look like his father, Lamech suspected that he had been sired by one of the incoming sons of God, so he (Lamech) sent his father, Methuselah, to the place where his grandfather Enoch had gone -- called Achuzan in *The Book of the Secrets of Enoch* (Jack 56) -- to find out the truth. Enoch said that the child was Lamech's and that he would survive the great punishment that would be inflicted on the earth when it would be washed from all corruption.

> And he (Lamech called his name Noah, saying, This same shall comfort us concerning our work and toil of our hands, because of the ground which the LORD has cursed (Gen. 5.29).

A New Mortal Coming

The ground (adamah) was the substance of which the body had been formed. After good and evil had been tasted, the ground had been cursed to bring forth thorns and thistles and man had been condemned to eat bread in the sweat of his face (which in the body represents the hormonal secretions from the pituitary gland). Noah, "settle, rest, quiet down, comfort," was a "just man (ish) and perfect in his generations." He represented the perfect specimen of a mortal through whom the line of Adam would enter the new stage of development in the earth. Now that the Spirit was to be withdrawn, Noah would generate the pattern for the new being and establish one of "the seven pillars hewn out of wisdom" (Prov. 9.1) the spiritual center in the body of the "holy place." And Noah was five hundred years old: and Noah begat Shem, Ham and Japheth (Gen. 6.10). While only the first sons were named among Adam's other descendants through Seth, all three of Noah's sons were named. Adam introduced the divided consciousness, which had been personified by Cain and Abel, and Noah introduced the three levels of consciousness that were personified by Shem, Ham and Japheth.

Noah is Chosen

The impending disaster that was prophesied by Enoch was coming to the earth universally from God, the First Cause in nature:

> The earth also was corrupt before GOD; and the earth was filled with violence.

> And GOD looked upon the earth, and behold, it was corrupt: for all flesh had corrupted his way upon the earth (Gen. 6.12).

Noah, who like Enoch was in touch with the Omnipresent level of Consciousness where there is no time, foresaw the destruction that was coming to the earth:

> GOD: The end of all flesh is come before me: for the earth is filled with violence through them: and behold, I will destroy (shachath: cast off) them with the earth (or from the earth).

> Make you an ark of gopher-wood: rooms (or nests) shall you make in the ark, and shall pitch it within and without with pitch.

> And this [is the fashion] which you shall make it [of]: The length of the ark [shall be] three hundred cubits (450 ft.), the breath of it fifty cubits (75 ft.), and the height of it thirty cubits (45 fit.).

A window (light)[1] shall you make to the ark,
and in a cubit (18 in.) shall you finish it above;
and the door of the ark shall you set in the
side thereof: [with] lower, second, and third
[stories] shall you make it (Gen. 12-26).

Symbology of the Ark

The ark Noah built symbolized the construction of a vehicle by
which the adamic race would be saved on the individual and universal
levels: the new pattern of consciousness in the earth. Compared to the
Great Pyramid, the three levels represented the King's Chamber, the
Queen's Chamber and the Subterranean Chamber.

The window (light) symbolized the point of contact with the light
spoken of by Jesus when he said:

> The light of the body is the eye: therefore,
> when your eye is single (united), you whole
> body is full of light: but when [your eye] is
> evil, your whole body also is full of darkness
> (Luke 11.34, Matt. 6.22-23).

The door of the ark symbolized the entrance to the inner consciousness, the door spoken of by Jesus when he said: "I am the door: by
me if any man enter in, he shall be saved, and shall go in and out and
shall find pasture" (John 10.9). It is also the same symbol as the
entrance to the Great Pyramid which was closed on the outside and had
been opened from within.

Survival of the Just

Noah knew that the impending destruction would be brought on
because of the corrupting of the way, misusing the creative force in
nature.

> GOD: And behold, I, even I, do bring a flood
> of waters upon the earth, to destroy (cast of)
> all flesh: wherein [is] the breath (ruwach:
> "spirit") of life, from under heaven: [and]

---

[1] Tsohar: "a light, dual, double light" from Tsahar: "to glisten, to press out oil,
make oil."

> everything that [is] in the earth shall die (gava:
> "breathe out, give up the spirit").

> But with you will I establish my covenant: and
> you shall come into the ark, you and your
> sons, and your wife, and your sons' wives with
> you. And of every living thing of all flesh, two
> of every [sort] shall you bring into the ark, to
> keep them alive with you: they shall be male
> (zakar) and female (negebah).

> Of fowls after their kind, and of cattle after
> their kind, of every creeping thing (reptile) of
> the earth (ground) after their kind: two of
> every [sort] shall come unto you to keep
> [them] alive.

> And take you unto you of all food that is
> eaten, and you shall gather it to you; and it
> shall be for food for you and for them (Gen.
> 6.17-21).

The flood coming on the universal level and the withdrawal of the spirit will apply to those below the heavenly level of consciousness. The covenant will be made with the new pattern.

Noah, who "walked with GOD" and "found grace in the eyes of the LORD" followed the Omnipresent Consciousness:

> Thus did Noah, according to all that GOD
> commanded him, so did he (Gen. 6.22).

This cleansing of the earth was coming on the universal level in Earth and the individual level in the body. Now Noah was instructed on the individual level:

> LORD: Come you and all your house into the
> ark: for thee I have seen righteous before me
> in this generation.

Of every clean beast you shall take to you by
sevens, the male (ish) and the female (ishshah): and of beasts that [are] not clean by
two, the male (ish) and his female (ishshah).

Of fowls of the air by sevens, the male (zakar)
and the female (negebah): to keep seed alive
upon the face of all the earth.

Yet for seven days, and I will cause it to rain
upon the earth forty days and forty nights: and
every living substance (or life still standing)
that I have made will I destroy (blot out) from
off the face of the earth (ground: adamah)
(Gen. 7.1-3).

Seven is a cyclic and spiritual number that refers to the inner man.
Every living substance made by the LORD represented the attributes
that had been named individually by the inner man. The seven pairs
(ish/ishshah) of clean beasts that Noah would take into the ark (the new
pattern) represented the purified physical attributes. The two pair of
"unclean" beasts represented the "unclean" physical desires that would
be left as a part of the new pattern of mortals, who were was recognized
as "also flesh." They also represented the Nephilim such as the
Rephaim, Horim, Emim, Anakim and Zamzumim, not of Noah's line,
who survived the flood and were considered "unclean." The fowls of the
air represented the thoughts, the mental realm.

And Noah did according unto all that the
LORD commanded him.

And Noah [was] six hundred years old when
the flood of waters was upon the earth (Gen.
7.5-6).

The first entrance of Noah and his family and the animals of the
ground into the ark symbolized the spiritual entrance into the new pattern:

And Noah went in, and his sons, and his wife,

and his sons' wives with him, into the ark,
because of the waters of the flood.

Of clean beasts, and of beasts that [are] not
clean and of fowls, and of every thing that
creeps upon the earth (ground: adamah).

There went in two and two unto Noah into the
ark, the male (zakar) and the female (negebah), as GOD had commanded Noah.

And it came to pass after seven days (or on the
seventh day), that the waters of the flood were
upon the earth (Gen. 7. 7-9).

The seven days spend in the ark before the rain came was a repeat of
the seven days of creation before the LORD GOD had caused it to rain
on the earth (Gen. 2.5). The second entrance of Noah and his family
(this time his sons were named) and the animals of the earth into the ark
represented the actual entrance:

In the six hundredth year of Noah's life, in the
second month, the seventeenth day of the
month, the same day were all the fountains of
the great deep broken up, and the windows
(floodgates) of heaven were opened.

And the rain was upon the earth forty days
and forty nights.

In the self-same day entered Noah, and Shem,
and Ham, and Japheth, the sons of Noah, and
Noah's wife, and the three wives of his sons
with them, into the ark:

They, and every beast (life) after his kind, and
all the cattle after their kind, and every creeping thing that creeps upon the earth after his
kind, and every fowl after his kind, every bird

of every sort (or wing).

And they that went in, went in male and female of all flesh, as GOD had commanded him: and the LORD shut him in (Gen. 7.10-16).

When the Lord shut Noah in, symbolically, the Comforter, the peace of the Holy Spirit, and the spiritual being was shut in the new pattern. In the Great Pyramid, this is symbolized as the door that is shut from the outside, but which was opened from the inside.

And the flood was forty days upon the earth and the waters increased, and bare up the ark, and it was lift up above the earth.

And the waters prevailed, and were increased greatly upon the earth: and the ark went upon the face of the waters.

And the waters prevailed exceedingly upon the earth: and all the high hills that [were] under the whole heaven were covered.

Fifteen cubits (25 ft.) upward did the waters prevail: and the mountains (or range of hills) were covered.

And all flesh died (gava: "breathed out, gave up the spirit") that moved upon the earth, both of fowl and of cattle, and of beast (life), and of every creeping thing that creeped upon the earth (erets) and every man (adam).

All in whose nostrils [was] the breath (nesh-ama: vital breath) of life, of all that [was] in the dry [land] or desert (charabah) died (muwth: "die, lit. or fig.") (Gen. 7.17-22).

End of the original adamic being, the first root race, and withdrawal of the spirit from all those below the heavenly level of consciousness had now come, as all flesh that moved upon the earth gave up the spirit, and all in whose nostrils was the vital breath died.

> And every substance was destroyed (blotted out) which was upon the face of the ground (adamah), both man and cattle and creeping things (swarms of minute animals), and fowl of the heaven; and they were destroyed (blotted out) from the earth; and Noah only remained [alive] and they that were with him in the ark.

> And the waters prevailed upon the earth an hundred and fifty days (Gen. 7.23-24).

The old pattern had now been erased from the earth. Withdrawal of the spirit from those who were not perfect in their use of the Creative Force as Noah had been, and the destruction of that current civilization and the ungodly, was symbolized as the first destruction. The blotting out of the old pattern universally was symbolized as the second destruction. Only Noah (just man) and those who were with him in the ark (the new pattern) remained. Most cultures have legends of a world-wide deluge that occurred because humans had become so wicked that God destroyed them and began again with only a few survivors. In the Greek story, Deucalion and his wife, Pyrrha, survived the deluge in a boat that landed on Mt. Parnassus and became the ancestors of the renewed race. In the Hindu story, Vaivasvata built a vessel and saved his family and plants and animals. His boat rested on Mt. Himalaya. In the Persian story in the Zend-Avesta, Yima, the shepherd, built a boat and saved the animals.

That the coming deluge, which would wipe out and erase the old pattern, was known universally is alluded to by Peter:

> By [the Spirit, Christ] went and preached unto the spirits in prison;

> Which sometime were disobedient when once the long-suffering of God waited in the days of

Noah, while the ark was a preparing... (1 Pet.
3.19-20)

A story that is very close to Noah's is the Babylonian account in the
Eleventh Tablet of the "Epic of Gilgamesh" in *Documents form Old
Testament Times* (Thomas 19-24). In this story, Utnapishti: Lord of
Shuruppak, was told by the gods to abandon his riches, seek out all
living kind, destroy his house and build a vessel to exact specifications
by which to survive the flood. In the Babylonian flood story, Utnapishti's boat rested on Mount Nisir:
As with most of the flood stories, the survivors assumed that all of
mankind except them had been destroyed. The Greek, Persian, Hindu
and Babylonian flood stories could conceivably have been versions of
Noah's story since his descendants eventually scattered into the sur-
rounding countries, but that does not account for the deluge stories of
the Pacific and the Americas that also tell of a world-wide flood and
chosen survivors.
Although legends of the other branches of mankind tell of survivors
of a world-wide deluge, just as they tell of the sons of God and their first
man, as Adam biblically symbolized the primal man and all the sons of
God, Noah and the seven members of his family symbolized survival of
the righteous in the earth and represented the new pattern in the line of
Adam:

(GOD) spared not the old world, but saved
Noah the eighth (person) a preacher of righteousness, bringing in the flood upon the
world of the ungodly (2 Pet. 2.5).

(In the ark) few, that is eight souls were saved
by water. The like figure whereunto baptism
does also now save us... (1 Pet. 3.20-21)

In the body, the path of spiritual impulses on the endocrine system
forms a figure eight like the double helix of the DNA spiral. The flow
from the pituitary crosses over to one of the reproductive glands then to
the other, rises, crosses over and reunites with the pituitary. The eight
souls saved by water represent the new pattern, the way of salvation
individually (physical and spiritual baptism) and collectively as the
macrocosm of the DNA spiral. Greek and Egyptian legends of the eight
"gods" out of whom came the twelve gods, parallel the story of Noah:

out of the eight survivors of Adam's line eventually came the twelve Tribes of Israel after the new order was established.

Symbology
6. End of the Beginning

NOAH - The settled pattern of mortal man chosen to survive for the next step in the physical evolution.

THE ARK - Pattern of the inner vehicle by which the man would be saved on the individual and universal level.

THREE LEVELS OF THE ARK - New pattern of the three higher levels of consciousness in the body.

WINDOW IN THE ARK - Point of contact with the light.

DOOR - Entrance to inner consciousness.

SEVEN PAIRS OF CLEAN BEASTS - New pattern of the purified consciousness in the physical.

TWO PAIRS OF UNCLEAN BEASTS - "Unclean" physical desires that would remain as part of the new pattern and the Nephilim who survived the flood.

FOWLS - Thoughts, the mental realm.

SEVEN DAYS BEFORE RAINS CAME - Period of gestation of the new pattern comparable to the seven days of creation by God before the Lord God caused it to rain on the ground.

FORTY DAYS IN THE ARK - Testing period of the new pattern.

EIGHT SOULS SAVED - The new physical pattern.

7. The New Order

Compared with the symbology of the Great Pyramid, when the ark was lifted above the earth and went on the face of the waters, the new pattern of the race was raised up out of the well shaft. When the ark rested on top of the mountains of Ararat, the new pattern was at the top of the Great Pyramid from which it descended into the earth.

The Ark Rested

> And GOD remembered Noah, and every living thing, and all the cattle that [was] with him in the ark: and GOD made a wind (spirit) to pass over the earth, and the waters assuaged.
>
> The fountains also of the deep, and the windows of heaven were stopped, and the rain from heaven was restrained.
>
> And the waters returned from off the earth continually and after the end of an hundred and fifty days the waters were abated.
>
> And the ark rested in the seventh month, on the seventeenth day of the month, upon the mountain of Ararat.
>
> And the waters decreased continually, until the tenth month: in the tenth [month], on the first [day] of the month, were the tops of the mountains seen (Gen. 8. 1-5).

The seventh month represented the spiritual completion and the tenth month (a numerological one) represented the new beginning.

In the Babylonian flood story, on the seventh day Utnapishti freed a dove that came back to him, then he sent out a swallow that also came back. So he sent out a raven, which did not return.

The Raven and the Dove

While Utnapishti sent out three birds: a dove, a swallow, and a raven, Noah sent out two:

And it came to pass at the end of forty days, that Noah opened the window (challown - perforated window).

And he sent forth a raven, which went forth to and fro, until the waters were dried up from off the earth.

Also he sent forth a dove from him, to see if the waters were abated off the face of the ground.

But the dove found no rest for the sole of her foot, and she returned unto him into the ark; for the waters [were] on the face of the whole earth. Then he put forth his hand, and took her and pulled her in unto him (or caused her to come) into the ark.

And he stayed yet other seven days; and again he sent forth the dove out of the ark.

And the dove came into him in the evening, and lo, in her mouth was an olive-leaf pluckt off. So Noah knew that the waters were abated from off the earth.

And he stayed yet other seven days, and sent forth the dove; which returned not again unto him any more (Gen. 8.6-12).

The raven that Noah sent out of the window of the ark, which went to and fro until the waters were dried off the earth represented the darkness and was ominous of the adversary who would continually go to and fro in the earth. The dove that Noah sent from him represented the Spirit that had been withdrawn. The third time the dove went out and did not return was ominous of the withdrawal of the Spirit of the Lord from the new pattern. (The dove would return as the Holy Spirit that entered Jesus.)

Leaving the Ark

And it came to pass in the six hundredth and first year, in the first [month], the first [day] of the month, the waters were dried up from off the earth: and Noah removed the covering of the ark, and looked and behold, the face of the ground was dry.

And in the second month, on the seven and twentieth day of the month, was the earth dried (Gen. 8.13-14).

The purification by water on the individual and universal levels had been completed and the just man was still in touch with the Omnipresent Consciousness:

GOD: Go forth of the ark, you, and your wife, and your sons, and your sons' wives with you.

Bring forth with you every living thing that is with you, of all flesh, [both] of fowl, and of cattle, and of every creeping thing that creeps upon the earth; that they may breed abundantly in the earth, and be fruitful, and multiply upon the earth (Gen. 8.16-17).

Adam's line had been transported to another area during the deluge. (The migration world-wide, via boats, during the deluge is indicated by the boat pits at the base of the Great Pyramid.) Now they disembarked in a new land:

And Noah went forth, and his sons, and his
wife, and his sons' wives with him:

Every beast (life), every creeping thing, and
every fowl, [and] whatsoever creeped upon the
earth, after their kinds, went forth out of the
ark (Gen. 18-19).

The First Altar

Lamech had said that Noah would bring comfort because of the
ground that the LORD had cursed. The highest spiritual center in the
body, the "most holy," the level of the pituitary, had been designated to
Adam. Noah's first act after leaving the ark was to build an altar to the
LORD, which symbolized the establishment in the new man of the
"holy place," the point of contact with the LORD, the spiritual center of
the Omniscient Consciousness, the seat of truth, the level of the pineal
gland.

And Noah builded an altar unto the LORD,
and took of every clean beast, and of every
clean fowl, and offered burnt-offerings on the
altar.

And the LORD smelled a sweet savor (or
savor of rest): and the LORD said in his heart,
I will not again curse the ground any more for
man's sake; for the imagination (or thought)
of man's heart is evil from his youth: neither
will I again smite any more every thing living,
as I have done.

While the earth remain (or as yet all the days
of the earth), seed-time, and harvest, and cold
and heat, and summer and winter, and day and
night shall not cease (Gen. 20.22).

By offering the clean beasts and fowl (the clean attributes) on this
altar, Noah established the spiritual center of the "holy place" (the
pineal). Literally, the significance of the burnt-offering is to appease
the animal appetites. Through the imagination and senses, the offering

becomes a real experience, much in the same way that the body reacts by salivating when a lemon is cut even though it is not eaten. An offering was also made in the Babylonian story of the flood.

The inner being (LORD) recognized that the imagination is evil, but because of the establishment of this center, the substance of which man was made (ground) would not be cursed again as Lamech had prophesied. However, as long as man remains in the earth he will experience duality symbolized by hot/cold, winter/summer, etc.).

The New Command

In Genesis One, the eternal images of God had been blessed to:

> Be fruitful, and multiply, and replenish the earth, and subdue it: and have dominion over the fish of the sea, and over the fowl of the air, and over every living thing that moves upon the earth: (Gen. 1.28).

That blessing had not been repeated in Genesis Two to the form of the physical man made from the dust of the ground by the LORD GOD (the attuned Omniscient Consciousness), because that being was the "multiplication." The adamic being had initiated a form of "multiplying" through the physical that became the inheritance of the race. The new order was now again blessed from the Omnipresent (GOD) level, but was not given the injunction to subdue the earth, because abusing the creative force in nature, "corrupting God's way," had been the downfall of the antediluvians.

> GOD: Be fruitful, and multiply, and replenish the earth.

> And the fear of you, and the dread of you, shall be upon every beast of the earth, and upon every fowl of the air, upon all that moves [upon] the ground and upon all the fishes of the sea; into your hand are they delivered.

> Every moving thing that lives shall be meat for you; even as the green herb have I given you all things.

> But the flesh with the life (nephesh: breathing
> creature, soul) thereof, [which is] the blood
> thereof, shall you not eat (Gen. 9.1-4).

The new order is given dominance over the animal kingdom in the
earth and the animal instincts in the body to be sustained by. Now, the
second root race that is more physical, will also be carnivorous, but is
warned against cannibalism and misuse of the animal instincts.

> And surely your blood of your lives (nephesh)
> will I require: at the hand of every beast (life)
> will I require it, and at the hand of man; at the
> hand of every man's brother will I require the
> life (nephesh) of a man.

> Whoso sheds man's blood, by man shall his
> blood be shed: for in the image of GOD made
> he man.

> And you, be you fruitful and multiply: bring
> forth abundantly in the earth, and multiply
> therein (Gen. 9.5-7).

The earth had been wiped clean and the new order began with a
clean slate. Divine Justice, reaping the rewards of ones actions was still
in effect in the world and in the body.

Covenant of the Rainbow
God had promised to establish a covenant with Noah and every living creature. The rainbow became the symbol of that covenant:

> GOD: And I, behold, I establish my covenant
> with you, and with your seed after you;

> And with every living creature that is with you,
> or fowl, of the cattle, and of every (life) of the
> earth with you, from all that go out of the ark,
> to every beast (life) of the earth.

And I will establish my covenant with you;
neither shall all flesh be cut off any more by
the waters of a flood; neither shall there any
more be a flood to destroy the earth.

GOD: This is the token (sign) of the covenant
which I make between me and you, and every
living creature with is with you, for perpetual
generations. I do set my bow in the cloud, and
it shall be for a token (sign) of a covenant between me and the earth.

And it shall come to pass, when I bring a cloud
over the earth, that the bow shall be seen in
the cloud:

And I will remember my covenant, which is
between me and you, and every living creature
of all flesh; and the waters shall no more
become a flood to destroy all flesh.

And the bow shall be in the cloud; and I will
look upon it, that I may remember the everlasting covenant between GOD and every living creature of all flesh that is upon the earth.

This is the token of the covenant which I have
established between me and all flesh that is
upon the earth (Gen. (Gen. 9.13-16).

This covenant made with the living creatures (the attributes of the
inner man on the earthly level) and all flesh will extend to the new order
individually in the body and collectively in the earth, as neither of these
floods will occur again. Bow, gesheth: "bending," is also "a bow for
shooting, or the iris -- the rainbow." In Greek mythology, Iris is the
goddess of the rainbow and messenger of the gods.

Individually, the bow set in the clouds represents the aura, the colors that Earth beings vibrate to according to the emotions registered in
the spiritual centers, i.e., red: anger, yellow: fear, blue: true, green: envy,
purple: regality, gold: good, etc. In a play on words, in The Revelation

the bow and arrow given to the first angel symbolizes the activating force from the first spiritual center.

The rainbow also stands between the being and God, between the finite and the infinite, until the heavenly level of consciousness is reached. In The Revelation when the door is opened in heaven and John goes immediately in the Spirit, there is a rainbow around the throne that he sees in heaven (Rev. 4:1-3). After the sixth trumpet sounds he sees an angel come down from heaven with a rainbow upon his head (Rev. 10:1).

Because of the rainbow, there will be no destruction by a flood again: actions will be remembered in the Omnipresent level of consciousness - God will look upon the bow and remember.

The Vineyard

The beginning in the earth of the adamic race had been symbolized as a garden planted by the LORD GOD in the east of Eden. The new beginning of the post-diluvian race was symbolized as a vineyard planted by Noah:

> And Noah began to be a husbandman, and he planted a vineyard:
>
> And he drank of the wine, and was drunken; and he was uncovered within his tent.
>
> And Ham, the father of Canaan, saw the nakedness of his father, and told his two brethren without.
>
> And Shem and Japheth took a garment, and laid it upon both his shoulders, and went backward, and covered the nakedness of their father: and their faces were backward, and they saw not their father's nakedness (Gen. 9.20-23).

Jesus compared the unified consciousness to the vine when he said, "I am the true vine and my Father is the husbandman" (John 15.1). As the husbandman and the father, Noah represented the source of the spiritual consciousness of the new order.

However, when Noah became drunk with the fruit of the vine he had planted, the spiritual man again became exposed and as a result was covered. Noah's three sons symbolized the three-dimensional consciousness:

> SHEM, "name, fame," symbolized the spiritual, the superconscious which attunement of the Ominiscient Consciousness [LORD] and the Omnipresent Consciousness [GOD] is made to reach the superconscious mind, the collective consciousness.

> JAPHETH, "expand," symbolized the mental, the intellect that will expand in the next evolutionary phase as the subconscious mind, the seat of truth, the book where man's individual record is written, the level of the Omniscient Consciousness.

> HAM, "hot," symbolized the physical, the conscious mind, the level where man can be deceptive, where he exercises free will in his use of the creative energy.

By overindulging in the wine (the symbolic spirit, the creative energy), and becoming drunk with its power, Noah changed his consciousness. When the conscious mind (symbolized by Ham) became aware of the source (the father) of the creative energy, that awareness was transmitted to the higher levels of consciousness (Shem and Japheth) and the source was concealed by the veil of the subconscious and superconscious minds. The awareness of that power was in the back of the head, literally and figuratively. A safeguard was now set up so that man would not be able to reach the source unless he penetrated the veil.

> And Noah awoke from his wine, and knew what his younger son had done unto him.

> And he said, "Cursed be Canaan: a servant of servants shall he be unto his brethren.

And he said, Blessed be the LORD GOD of Shem; and Canaan shall be his servant (or servant to them).

GOD shall enlarge (or persuade) Japheth and he shall dwell in the tents of Shem; and Canaan shall be his servant (Gen. 9.24-27).

Here the sins of the father are passed on to the son. It was Ham, not Canaan, who saw the nakedness of Noah, yet the curse was placed on Canaan. As a literal record from the perspective of hind sight, justification is being given for the genocide of the Canaanites by Joshua. As symbology related to the body, the boundary and limitations of the conscious mind were being set when Noah cursed Canaan to be a servant of servants to his brethren. Ham's son, Canaan: "Bring down low, humiliate, merchant, trafficker," represented the results of the misuse of free will: the limited consciousness and the fallen spiritual energy, which were now destined to serve the servants of his brethren, the five senses and the four lower, earth-related, centers of the spiritual body and relay the impressions from the conscious mind to subconscious and superconscious minds. Literally, descendants of Shem and Japheth will rely on merchants and traffickers.

The Earth is Divided

Loss of access to the kingdom of heaven and loss of communication between the earth forces in the body and in the earth took place during the days of Peleg, who was born 299 years after the flood.

And the whole earth was of one language (or boundary), and of one speech.

And it came to pass, as they journeyed from the east (or eastward), that they found a plain in the land of Shinar; and they dwelt there (Gen. 11.1-2).

Language, sepheth, also means "the lip (as a natural boundary)" by analogy, "margin, bank[1], boundary, boarder, edge," and conveys a dou-

---

[1] Compare sepheth, bank: Gen. 41.17, Det. 4.48, Jos. 12.2, 13.9, 16, 2 Ki. 2.13, Ezek. 47.7, 12, Dan. 12.5.

ble meaning here. Speech, dabar, is "word," by implication, "a matter, a cause, act." While Noah's descendants were all together in one location they had the same form of communication, but when they settled on the plain of Shinar, "two rivers, divided stream," the division was set in motion.

> And they said one to another, Go to, let us make brick, and burn them thoroughly (or to a burning). And they had brick for stone, and slime had they for mortar (Gen. 11.3).

Ham's grandson, Nimrod, began to be a mighty one in the earth and he was a mighty hunter before (in the face of) the LORD. He symbolized the attempt to seize the level of the Omniscient Consciousness through force of will. The beginning of his kingdom was Babel, Erech, Accad and Calneh, which were emblematic of the earthly kingdom, the four earth centers of the spiritual body.

Instead of naming the name by attuning their higher levels of consciousness, Noah's descendants attempted to build a city and a tower with its top in heaven and make a name. They were united in their effort through fear that they would be scattered upon the face of the earth. The concerted power of the negative emotion of fear registered on the bow stronger than their desire to reach "heaven" and they were rebuffed by the safeguard set up to prevent the new order from misusing the creative energy.

> And the LORD came down to see the city and the tower which the children (sons) of men builded.

> And the LORD said, Behold, the people [is] one, and they have all one language; and this they begin to do; and now nothing will be restrained from them, which they have imagined to do.

> Go to, let us go down, and there confound (mix) their language, that they may not understand one another's speech (language -- sepheth) (Gen. 11.5-7).

While the earth forces were in harmony, they were in communication at the level of the LORD. However, because Noah's descendants attempted to expand their consciousness by means other than attunement with GOD (they used the wrong materials: they had brick for stone and slime for mortar), they altered their consciousness and confusion and division occurred:

> So the LORD scattered them abroad from thence upon the face of all the earth: and they left off to build the city.

> Therefore is the name of it called Babel ("confusion, chaos"),[2] because the LORD did there confound the language of all the earth: and from thence did the LORD scatter them abroad upon the face of all the earth (Gen. 11.8-9).

Consciously, Noah's descendants had vainly thought that their purpose in the earth was to remain together and make a name, but when the purpose they had chosen was registered on the spiritual level collectively, the separate purposes, dictated by Divine Justice, became evident from the spiritual level. No longer able to call on the supernatural power of Spirit at will, the new order was now forced to live by reason. In the evolutionary process, emphasis shifted to the left side of the brain and development of the intellect. Contact with higher consciousness would now come through dreams and intuition from the night side as summed up by the Psalmist: "Day unto day utters speech, and night unto night shows knowledge: (Ps. 19.2).

Shift of emphasis from development of the physical to the development of the mental had been symbolized when Noah said to Shem, "Blessed be the LORD GOD of Shem" (Gen. 9.26), and to Japheth, "GOD shall enlarge Japheth and he shall dwell in the tents of Shem" (Gen. 9.27). Literally, Shem's descendants through Abraham will keep alive the spirituality and belief in the Lord God, which will be expanded to the gentiles, the descendants of Japheth.

The subconscious mind, which registers all of man's experiences, will expand as man develops the intellect. Since the carnal mind is enmity against God and not subject to the laws of God (Rom. 8.7), the

---

[2] Also "Gate of Bel, court of Baal," the Babylonian Lord·

conscious mind is denied direct access to the superconscious mind. Because the conscious mind is deceptive and serves only the physical being, the mental/spiritual (Japheth and Shem) becomes the door, the way of attunement. This had been indicated when Jesus said, "I AM the door," and later emphasized when he said, "I AM the way the truth and the life: no man comes to the Father but by me" (John 14.6). When the subconscious, the level of the Omniscient Consciousness expands spiritually, union with the superconscious, the level of the Omnipresent Consciousness will take place and one will dwell in the tents of Shem. At this level the Lord is one, i.e., this level is the point of contact, telepathically or through visions, of all souls with the Lords, or eternal spirits of all other souls, whether they are incarnate in the physical or out of the body.[3]

Jesus expounded worship of the Father in spirit and truth (John 4.23-24), not from the conscious mind to be seen of men, but in secret: by way of the subconscious mind. To this end he gave a prayer (Matt. 6.9-13), utilizing the symbols in Genesis: Father, heaven, earth, temptation, bread, and evil, by which one could properly unite the earth forces of the spiritual body and regain access to the level of spirit and truth in the kingdom of heaven within:

Our Father which art in heaven

> (Acknowledge the seventh spiritual center, seat of the pituitary, point of contact with the Omnipresent Consciousness, the superconscious mind.)

Hallowed be thy name.

> (Acknowledge the sixth spiritual center, level of the pineal, point of contact with and the subconscious mind where all actions are recorded truthfully, level of the Omniscient Consciousness, from which union with the Omnipresent Consciousness, the superconscious can be made.)

Thy kindgom come.

> (Awaken the spiritual level, the kingdom of God within.)

Thy will be done in earth as [it is] in heaven.

---

[3] See 2 Cor. 12.1-3, & Rev. 1.10, 4.2, 17.3, & 21.10.

(Awaken the fifth center, level of the thyroid, attune the physical and spiritual purposes.)

Give us this day our daily bread

(Awaken the first spiritual center, level of the reproductive organs, to receive the spiritual impulse, the bread that came down from heaven.)

And forgive us our debts as we forgive our debtors.

(Awaken of the third center, level of the solar plexsus, the adrenals, the enery that can be used constructively or destructively.)

And lead us not into [or keep us from][4] temptation,

(Awaken the second center of the lyden, the seat of imagination, the abdominal brain, the level of the fallen intellect, where the serpent had fallen -- protect us from misuse of the imaginative force.)

but deliver us from evil.

(Awaken the fourth center of the heart, the thymus, the seat of love/hate and immunity -- fill the heart with love.)

For thine is the kingdom, and the power, and the glory forever.

(Lift up the force through the three higher centers.)

Toward Mental Development

Journey of God's images in the earth from the creation to the division after the flood had covered a vast period of time as they travelled through various stages from the light in the beginning. These periods were covered in a prayer of Moses:

Lord, you have been our dwelling place in all generations.

Before the mountains were brought forth, or ever you had formed the earth and the world,

---

[4] LB reads: "do not let us enter into temptation,"

even from everlasting to everlasting, you are
God.

You turn man to destruction; and say, Return,
you children of men.

For a thousand years in your sight are but as
yesterday when it is past, and as a watch in the
night.

You carried them away with a flood; they are
as asleep; in the morning they are like grass
which grows up.

In the morning it flourishes, and grows up; in
the evening it is cut down and withers (Ps.
90.1-6)

The first stage in the earth plane of the sons of God was as spiritual
man, (the images of God) who manifested thought form bodies (sons of
men) and experienced good and evil. In the evolutionary process from a
"loosely knit" dust body toward modern man, the pattern originated in
the beginning had repeated: The light had manifested as the image
(Adam), who fathered, by his own will, sons of men (Cain and Abel),
who personified the dual consciousness. Misuse of the creative energy
resulted in destruction of the spiritual consciousness and the fallen son
of man. The individualized infinite consciousness (Abel) was reborn in
the physical by appointment of God and was a son of man who was a son
of God (Seth). The dual consciousness that Cain and Abel personified
became a permanent part of man's nature with the birth of Seth's son,
Enos, "mortal man."

The new-order mortals personified by the combination of Ham,
Shem and Japheth were truly three dimensional beings in the physical:
body, mind and spirit, conscious, subconscious and superconscious
minds, but the Spirit had been withdrawn. They would now live by their
wits and the developing intellect.

Noah lived to be nine hundred and fifty years old, and his line continued through his three sons, whose offspring scattered into surround-
ing nations. Their genealogies are listed in Chapter Ten which ends:

and by these were the nations (goy, "gentiles, foreign nations") divided (cachar: "profited (from trade) merchandise").

Now that the physical evolution of Homo sapiens was completed, the mental development would unfold from Abraham to Jesus, the last Adam, who would return to the first state of light.

In both the theories of creation and evolution, and the Biblical story, creation had come from the First Cause and physical evolution had come on the planet. The beginning of all had been light.

Symbology
7. The New Order

THE RAVEN - The adversary that goes to and fro in the Earth.

THE DOVE - The spirit, the Comforter.

THE FIRST ALTAR - Holy place, level of the Lord and the pineal in the body.

THE RAINBOW - The aura and the colors of the seven centers of the body.

THE VINEYARD - The source of spiritual consciousness of the new order.

SHEM - The spiritual level where attunement with superconsciousness can take place.

JAPHETH - The mental, subconscious mind.

HAM - The physical, the conscious mind.

CANAAN - Results of the fallen creative energy in the body and in the earth.

Bibliography

Bruckhardt, Titus. *Alchemy.* London, Stuart & Watkins, 1967.

Budge, Wallis. *Gods of the Egyptians.* New York: Dover Publications, 1969

Encyclopaedia Britannica. Chicago, 1953.

Fix, William R. *Pyramid Odyssey* . New York: Mayflower Books, 1978).

Franck, Adolphe. *The Kabbalah, The Religious Philosophy of the Hebrews.* New York: Bell Publishing Company, 1940.

Gaster, Theodor H. *The Dead Sea Scriptures.* Garden City, NY: Anchor Books, Anchor Press/Doubleday 1956.

Gore, Rick, Sr. Editor. "The Dawn of Human Neanderthals." *National Geographic* January 1996: Vol. 189, No. 1.

Hartman, Louis F., Trans. *Encyclopedic Dictionary of the Bible.* New York, McGraw-Hill, 1963.

Herodotus. *The Histories.* Translated by Aubrey de Selincourt. Baltimore, MD: Penguin Books, 1954.

Jack, Alexander, Trans. *The Book of the Secrets of Enoch.* Albuquerque, NM: Star Point Pub., Inc., 1972.

Josephus, Flavius. *The Complete Works of Josephus.* Translated by Whiston, William A. M. Grand Rapids, MI: Kregel Publications, 1960.

Laurence, Richard, Trans. *The Book of Enoch The Prophet.* Minneapolis, MN: Wizards Bookshelf, 1976.

Lost Books of The Bible (The). New American Library, New York, 1974.

Matt, Daniel Chanan, Trans. *Zohar, The Book of Enlightenment.* Ramsey, NJ: Paulist Press, 1983.

Mercatante, Anthony S. *Who's Who in Egyptian Mythology.* New York: Clarkson N. Potter, Inc., 1978.

New York Times. 11/8/81, p. 7.

Pliny (C. Plinius Secundus). *The Natural History.* Translated by Philemon Holland. New York: McGraw-Hill, 1964.

Rele, Vasant G. Rele. *The Mysterious Kundalini.* Bombay, India: D. B. Taraporevala Sons & Co., Ltd., undated.

Steiger, Brad. *Parade.* May 20, 1979.

Thomas, D. Winton, Ed. *Documents from Old Testament Times.* New York: Harper & Row, 1958.

Tompkins, Peter. *Secrets of the Great Pyramid.* New York: Harper and Row, 1971.

Walker, Charles. *Wonders of the Ancient World.* New York: Crescent Books, 1980.

Glossary of Symbols

ABEL - Transitory spiritual consciousness.

ALTAR - Holy place, level of the Lord and the pineal in the body.

ARK - Pattern of the inner vehicle by which the man would be saved on the individual and universal level.

ARK, THREE LEVELS - New pattern of the three higher levels of consciousness in the body.

ARK, WINDOW - Point of contact with the light.

BEAST OF THE FIELD - Animal instincts.

BABEL - Confusion.

BREAD - Spirit and life in the physical.

BREATH OF LIFE - Vital breath, intelligent activating spirit.

CAIN - Fixed physical consciousness fallen in the Earth.

CANAAN - Results of the fallen creative energy in the body and in the earth.

CHERUBIM - Animal instincts in the physical that separate man from the source of eternal life: desire for propagation, sustenance, self-preservation and self-gratification.

COATS OF SKINS - Second change in the evolving "dust" body and the developing cerebellum concerned with muscle coordination.

CURSE ON THE MAN - Submergence of the source of eternal life in the body until the return to the original state. (Literally - Mental anguish, pain and disease, and survival by the physical.)

CURSE ON THE SERPENT - Fall of the mental/physical to the abdominal brain.

CURSE ON THE WOMAN - Subduing of the intuition as long as the mental rationale is predominant. (Literally - Physical reproduction and menopause.)

DARKNESS - The rebellious force, the anti-light, the anti-Christ Consciousness.

DAUGHTERS OF MEN - Manifestations of the created.

DAY - The state of consciousness of the Light.

DOOR of the ark - Entrance to inner consciousness.

DOVE - The spirit, the Comforter.

DUST of the ground - Molecular construction.

EARTH - The physical level of consciousness, the ground of life in the physical and the physical level of consciousness in the body.

EDEN - Original estate of the source of consciousness that was lost.

ENOCH - Initiation into the spiritual development.

ENOS - Mortal man seeking contact with the inner man.

EUPHRATES - Discernment, sense of smell and predominant expression of the brown division of the race.

FLAMING SWORD - Creative energy that can be used in either direction.

FRUIT OF CAIN - Undesirable actions.

FIG LEAVES - First change in the evolving "dust" body, the leaf-like foldings, the lamellae, of the cerebellum. Psychologically, defense mechanism for suppressing memory.

FOUR HEADS OF THE RIVER THAT WENT OUT OF EDEN. - Four divisions of the original consciousness dispersed in the world and in the body as forms of sense expressions of four other divisions of the race.

FRUIT OF THE TREE - Activities and rewards of the constructive and destructive forces.

FOWL OF THE AIR - Mental attributes.

GARDEN EASTWARD IN EDEN - Original site of consciousness, source of the purposes in the body individually and collectively in the world.

GIHON - Sustaining force, sense of taste, predominant expression of the black division of the race.

GOD - The Omnipresent Consciousness, the First Cause in nature, the Creator, the Infinite Mind.

GROUND (Adamah) - Elements found in Earth.

HAM - The physical, the conscious mind.

HEAVEN - The spiritual level of consciousness in the body.

HERBS - Sustaining and healing forces within.

HIDDEKEL - Force of perception, sense of sight, predominant expression of the white division of the race.

JAPHETH - The mental, the subconscious mind.

LIGHT - The Omniscient Consciousness, the Constructive Force, the First-born, the Son, the Word, the Lord, the Christ Consciousness, the Master.

LINE OF CAIN - Initiation of development of materiality.

LINE OF SETH - Development toward initiation of spirituality.

LORD - The Omniscient Consciousness, the Son, the image of God within, the I, the ego, the soul, the spiritual body.

LORD GOD - The Omniscient Consciousness in attunement with the Omnipresent Consciousness, the I AM.

MAN (Ish) - Active principle, logic and reason.

MAN A LIVING SOUL - Homo sapiens containing the inner spiritual body the image of God, the Son of God.

MAN FORMED FROM THE DUST OF THE GROUND BY THE LORD GOD - The Ideal physical form for homo sapiens made by the LORD, the image, in attunement with GOD, the Creator.

MANKIND IN THE IMAGE OF GOD - Spiritual Sons of God, creations of the Creator, the spiritual body.

MARK OF CAIN - Creative ability through the hands and the five senses.

MIST - The water, the source of life, the hormones.

NEPHILIM - Thought form creations of the created.

NIGHT - The state of unconsciousness of the Light.

NOAH - The settled pattern of mortal man chosen to survive for the next step in the physical evolution.

OFFERING OF ABEL - Desirable actions.

PISON - Balance, sense of hearing, predominant expression of the yellow division of the race.

PLANTS - Thought formations that manifest as actions.

RAINBOW - The aura and the colors of the seven centers of the body.

RAVEN - The adversary that goes to and fro in the Earth.

RIVER THAT WENT OUT OF EDEN - Original stream of consciousness of the total body, sense of feeling individually in the body and collectively in the world, predominant expression of the red division of the race.

SETH - Rebirth of the spiritual consciousness in the physical.

SERPENT - Deceptive mental/physical rational.

SEVEN PAIRS OF CLEAN BEASTS - New pattern of the purified consciousness in the physical.

SHEM - The spiritual level where attunement with superconsciousness can take place.

SONS OF GOD - Creations of the creator. SONS OF MEN - Creations of the created, thought form manifestations of the Sons of God.

SPIRIT OF GOD - The Omnipotent Consciousness, the Activating Force.

STARS - Expressions of the Light Consciousness in the heavenly level that are reflected in the physical consciousness as basic patterns of activity.

THORNS AND THISTLES - Unproductive thoughts, actions and offspring.

TREES THAT GREW OUT OF THE GROUND - Basic patterns of action, purposes and functions of the inner man individually and collectively.

TREE OF LIFE - The autonomic nervous system in the body, wisdom and understanding of the unified consciousness.

TREE OF THE KNOWLEDGE OF GOOD AND EVIL - Constructive and destructive forces in the body and in the world previously known by the inner man.

TWO GREAT LIGHTS - Rulers of the two levels of consciousness, the sun and moon consciousness, mental and emotional.

VINEYARD - The source of spiritual consciousness of the new order.

WATER - Nurturing source of life on the spiritual and physical levels.

WOMAN (Ishshah) - Receptive principle, intuition and emotion.